A Crime-Free Nation

What is morally right can differ drastically from what is considered lawful.

By

Roldimy Montinar

INFINITY PUBLISHING.COM

ISBN 0-7414-5329-0

Published by:

INFINITY
PUBLISHING.COM

1094 New DeHaven Street, Suite 100
West Conshohocken, PA 19428-2713
Info@buybooksontheweb.com
www.buybooksontheweb.com
Toll-free (877) BUY BOOK
Local Phone (610) 941-9999
Fax (610) 941-9959

Printed in the United States of America

Published October 2010

In Loving Memory Of:

Jarol Montinar
R.J. Montinar
Nicolas Montinar
Wally Montinar
Jacob Montinar
Saladin Ade

Introduction

Every intentional criminal act is subject to prosecution.

- Roldimy Montinar

While interest in crime has always been high, understanding why it occurs and what to do about it has always been a problem. Public officials and the criminal justice system personnel continue to offer simple and incomplete solutions for obliterating crime.

Criminology needs all the help it can get to explain and control criminal behavior. Crime itself is an intentional act in violation of the criminal law committed without defense or excuse, and penalized by the state as a felony or misdemeanor. Criminal behavior, therefore, is intentional behavior that violates a criminal code. Intentional means that the behavior did not occur accidentally or under duress. To be held responsible, a person must have known what they were doing during the criminal act and must have known that it was wrong. Now, should we restrict ourselves to a legal definition and talk only about those individuals who have been convicted of a crime? Or should we include individuals who indulge in anti-social behaviors, but have not been detected by the criminal justice system? If we abide strictly by the legal definition of crime and base discussion only on those people who have committed crime, do we consider as criminals or lawbreakers only those who have been convicted and incarcerated or do we include those who have probably broken the criminal law, but are not convicted?

A criminal is by definition one that has been detected, arrested, and convicted. However, we encounter problems when we limit ourselves to simply talk about persons legally defined as criminals and to consider and go beyond who are really criminals. Therefore, do we consider as lawbreakers just those who committed unlawful acts and were arrested and prosecuted or those who broke the law, but went undetected? Do we consider as innocent those who really committed a crime and were prosecuted, but were acquitted, or do we consider as criminal those who truly did not commit a crime they were convicted of? Do we consider as non-criminal a person who committed murder, but went undetected? Do we consider as innocent a person who truly committed murder, was prosecuted, but was acquitted? Do we consider as criminal a person who was wrongly prosecuted for murder and was convicted? Isn't at the same time that a person breaks the criminal law that they commit an unlawful act whether they were detected or not? Or do we only consider as committing an unlawful act a person who broke the criminal law and was prosecuted and convicted? Do we consider it okay for a person to engage in violating the criminal law as long as he went undetected?

Many countries around the world differ significantly in their criminal codes and are continually reversing them. What is morally wrong may not be considered as an unlawful act. What is considered unlawful in one country can also be a criminal act in another one, but the statutes (their way of prosecuting), the court system, process, and procedure may be different.

Many of us do not know the criminal law; therefore, we may, on certain occasions, violate a criminal code without knowing. Some who may know the criminal law seems not to know it very well by memory. Many times, when someone is about to do something and is considering whether it is lawful or not, the chances are, they will not have the criminal codes in front of them to make the determination. That may lead the person unable to decide and go ahead and do it anyway, hoping that it is lawful.

Many people were arrested and were prosecuted for violating the law when they did not really know that their act was unlawful and which statutes stated so. The problem is because the criminal judicial prosecution system and the law enforcement personnel presume and assume that we all know the law. Shouldn't it be that before someone is arrested and prosecuted for violating a criminal code that that determination should be made whether he knows that the act was unlawful? Why get someone arrested and prosecuted for committing an unlawful act, which they really did not know was in violation of the criminal law? How can a person know that they are violating the criminal law if they do not know the criminal statutes in the first place? If in order for a person to be held criminally responsible for breaking the law, he has to know that what he was doing was wrong and/or unlawful. If so, then how can a person be held criminally responsible for committing an unlawful act without anybody being able to prove he knew the criminal code? How can a person know what they were doing was unlawful if they did not know the criminal statutes? Nevertheless, the criminal judicial prosecution system has people prosecuted for committing unlawful acts with the assumption and the presumption that they know the criminal statutes. Knowing that what you were doing was lawful or not may not save you from criminal prosecution.

One can argue that it's wrong. Many criminal defense lawyers know that even when it might be the case, but telling the court that a defendant did not know that what he was doing was unlawful may not always be the best defense and can trigger to the admittance of some guilt.

Prosecutors may tell you that not prosecuting people for breaking the criminal law for the simple fact that they did not know what they were doing was unlawful will lead to many people taking advantage of it and taking it for granted.

Moreover, one of the most important things they know they have to do is to act as if they did not know what they were doing was unlawful for the simple fact that they did not know the criminal statutes. Some will try to take advantage of it even when they did in fact know that what they were doing was unlawful in the first place. That makes sense. But to prosecute a person criminally for assuming and presuming that he knew what he was doing was wrong, a determination has to be made that he truly knew the criminal law.

In order to make sure that everyone knows the criminal statutes and to get them prosecuted for committing an unlawful act, a way must be provided to everyone to learn and know the criminal statutes. It could be by way of radio, TV, giving free courses, or free books to everyone; all of those things can help. It is up to those in charge to know and think about how they can effectively and successfully do it. However, it must be a mandatory way of making sure that people know the criminal statutes, so when someone is prosecuted for violating the criminal law, there will be no room for excuses of not knowing. Once a mandatory way is provided, everyone can willfully and voluntarily participate and get to know and learn the criminal statutes but may not have to participate if they do not want to. However, at least a way to learn the criminal statutes is provided to them. Therefore, when a person is prosecuted for committing an unlawful act, it would no longer be that he did not know the criminal statutes to know that what he was doing was unlawful, but that he chooses not to know it. And the saying of, "I did not know that was unlawful," may no longer be a defense.

Another reason it is important is that the criminal statutes go to ever-changing statutes. Therefore, people need to be up-to-date about the criminal statutes.

Every society wants to be crime free. Somehow, crime free may mean bad news to some criminal defense lawyers. They will have no clients and make no money. That does not mean that some lawyers do not want their society to be crime free, but they know that considering their profession, there has to be crime for them to make money. Some lawyers in their society know that when crime rates are low, they make little money, and when crime rates are high, they are more likely to make more money considering how many people will walk into their office with a new criminal case. I strongly believe that in every society, a way must be provided to everybody to learn and know the criminal statutes. Will that help with the prevention of crime? I believe that it will make more sense and be fair to everyone who is involved.

Many people who were arrested, prosecuted, and convicted for committing the criminal law really did not know that they were violating the criminal law when they committed the unlawful act. One of the things every single one of us can do to help with the prevention of crime is to not violate the criminal law ourselves. Everyone is presumed and assumed to know their legal rights, but some really do not know what their legal rights are. I believe that a way must be provided to everyone to know their legal rights so that one day, they may not become victims of not knowing their legal rights. One can argue that a person who violates the criminal law, but truly did not know that his act was unlawful and was prosecuted by assuming that he knew the criminal statutes is a victim of not knowing the criminal codes. Therefore, something must be done so that no one is, becomes, and continues to be victims of not knowing the criminal statutes and their legal rights.

What is morally right can differ drastically from what is lawful.

Some people, when committing a criminal act, try to destroy evidence at the scene and think that they will escape prosecution. However, they fail to understand that other than evidence, there are other factors that can link them to the crime and lead to their arrest and conviction. When investigating a crime, law enforcement officers and personnel do not only search for evidence, but they go beyond that. They also look for links, connections, motives, and anything that might have something to do with the crime. They search for anything that can and may link a suspect to the crime and anything that may lead to an arrest. Therefore, it would be foolish for anyone to assume that destroying crime scene evidence would make a criminal act go undetected and escape prosecution.

Members of every society and consequently every society's judicial system perceive and process violators of the criminal statutes with some discrimination, so that the offender's background, personality, motivation, age, race, and legal counsel, as well as the circumstances surrounding the offense, all may affect the legal process. It is likely that individuals who have been arrested, convicted, and incarcerated represent a distinctly different sample from those who participate in illegal activity and perform unlawful acts but avoid detection, conviction, or incarceration. Not all those who are arrested go to trial. Criminals go through a process. A label of suspect is put on them. The criminal judicial prosecution system and/or the law enforcement personnel may decide that the person should be arrested. The arrested party may be charged with a crime at which point he becomes a defendant. The defendant may be tried and convicted, and then becomes a criminal. That is considering the legal definition of a criminal. The convicted person may be incarcerated in a correctional facility and be labeled a convict, inmate, prisoner, or a criminal. However, many people who truly commit a crime are filtered out for a variety of reasons. Everyone who is charged with a crime and was prosecuted and faced with a jury trial know well that whether they have truly committed the crime or not, their determination of guilt or innocence is to be determined by the jury. That is one of the reasons that the defendant in criminal cases sometimes are very nervous when the time comes for their verdict, even when they know that they are truly innocent. At least they know they are, but they are not making that determination; they can only help prove it.

Sometimes, even when it is proven that they are innocent, that may not help them to get a not guilty verdict. For as long as the determination of guilty is to be determined by a jury in a criminal case, it can be a questionable verdict considering what the verdict is contrary to what really happened will continue to dominate some criminal cases. The jurors were not witnesses of what truly happened as it happened, but they are presented with evidence, they listen to testimonies, they hear witnesses and other factors used in jury criminal trial to make their determination and vote for a verdict according to what they truly believe. What they believe and make their determination upon can be contrary to what really happened and that may result in an unfair verdict.

After voting, many jurors continue to ask themselves if their determination was fair and consistent to what really happened. Did they let somebody walk away free for a crime they truly committed? Did they have somebody convicted for a crime they are truly innocent of? It is generally acknowledged, therefore, that incarcerated individuals are not representative of the true criminal population. Consequently, if we discuss only legally determined criminals, we will be neglecting a considerable segment of the population that actually breaks the law.

We must continue to thank the law enforcement and the criminal justice system personnel for all their great effort and services and to continue to support and help them to always be successful on the difficult job and task they have to do day-by-day and with the prevention of criminal acts. They continue to put their life on the line every day to protect ours. Let's give them credit for that and let them know that we appreciate them. They truly deserve it. I personally thank them and congratulate them. Salute!

NOTE:

Because every society has a different and changing set of values, what may be judged a criminal act in one may not meet the criteria in another or even in the same society at a later time. Many countries differ significantly in their criminal codes and are continuously revising them. In this book, what may be relevant in one society may not be so in the other. This book is not giving anybody any legal advice nor is it intended to do so and nor is it the replacement of legal counsel. Anybody with legal needs, needs legal advice, or needs legal representation should consult a lawyer.

I am just sharing my ideas with you. You do not have to agree with the content of this book and there is always room for discussion. Whether you decide to do or follow anything you read in this book depends on your own free will to do so. This book is not asking or advising anyone to do or follow any content in it. This is not a law book and it should never be used for that purpose. This book is not in any way intended to offend or target anyone nor is it intended to accuse or point a finger at anyone and should never be used for those purposes. This book is not a law book and is not giving anyone legal advice and should not be used for those purposes. Anyone who needs advise on any kind of issue should consult whom they believe and know is the appropriate person to handle their business. This book is not giving any advice whatsoever to anyone and should never be used for that purpose.

Chapter 1

Crime

Some defendants hate the criminal justice system only to appreciate it when they become victim of a crime.

-Roldimy Montinar

Crime. It's being committed these days. It occurs often and it's happening around the world.

We are all capable of violating the criminal law in one way or another. The fact is that crime is a violation of the criminal law, and there must be a way to prosecute and punish those who commit unlawful acts and give justice to the victims.

The criminal judicial system is there for that reason. Even when to my understanding there is a system in place to punish those who violate the law, it does not stop certain individuals to commit unlawful acts. Even when the system provides stiff penalties and the ultimate sentence for those who commit serious crimes, people continue to break the law. Many of us have sometimes asked ourselves, *Is the criminal judicial system really working in to prevent people from committing unlawful acts?* I do believe that it is a good thing that there is a system in place to prosecute those who violate the criminal law. However, it is my understanding that not all individuals who violate the criminal law are prosecuted. The criminal law does not take action against those who violate it. Can you imagine how the world would be if there was no system to prosecute those who violate the criminal law where anybody could have committed crimes and walk? Where anyone could have given justice how they wanted?

We all have our own sense of justice. We want justice to be done our way. Our way of seeing justice being done and given may sometimes go beyond what the criminal judicial system considers and states as justice. I'm afraid that we sometimes think that our way in each situation is the best way to give justice, but we all have to go by what the law says and justice has to be given according to the law, regardless of how we think it should have been given.

If every single crime could have been prematurely prevented, then the criminal justice system would have no longer been necessary.

I must say that the criminal justice system protects a lot of us from wrongdoing and crime. While that does not mean that we will automatically be protected or not be victims of unlawful acts, it does give us a way of seeking justice if we believe that we become victims of it. There is not a day without crime being committed around the world. In addition, one of the reasons crime happens is because we are all able and capable of violating the criminal law intentionally or not. Violent crimes draw attention and sometimes anger people. Can you imagine the nightmare of a neighborhood being put on alert that there is a violent criminal on the loose?

We must give the law enforcement officers and personnel a lot of credit for putting their lives on the line day-by-day to protect ours, and to serve us and to protect us from wrongdoing and crime.

Can you imagine how your neighborhood would be if there were no law enforcement officers to go after those who commit crime? And when you become a victim of a crime that there is nobody you can call or turn to for help? You're on your own and regardless, there will be no justice given. How would you feel if you had to continuously be a victim of crime and know that there is nobody you can call to report the crime to and that unlawful acts will not be prosecuted? When it comes to facing justice, some hate the criminal justice system only to appreciate it when they become a victim of a crime.

Criminal lawbreakers have proved that every single crime cannot be prevented.

When some people are accused of a crime, they hate the criminal justice system because they do not want to be prosecuted for their unlawful acts. However, they seem to admire it when it is being used to give them justice for a crime they become a victim of. The criminal justice system continues to prosecute and sentence offenders for their unlawful acts, yet people continue to violate the criminal law. Therefore, can you imagine how it would be without the criminal justice system to prosecute offenders of unlawful acts? What would it mean to those who have no regard and respect for the criminal law? Sometimes, courts are overloaded with criminal cases and prisons are full with inmates, but people continue to break the law even when they know it will give them a ticket straight to jail. Some who come out of jail find their way right back in for violating the criminal law again. Newspapers, TV, and radios continuously report crime and their consequences to the offenders, yet crime keeps on happening and people continue to be victims of it. Law enforcement officers and personnel are on the streets and make their presence known, but that does not stop some individuals from breaking the law. Despite arrests, prosecutions, convictions, and sentences, the criminal law is being broken every single day. Sometimes, we cannot prevent crimes from happening and even when those who commit them are held responsible and prosecuted to the full extent of the law, they continue to break the law anyway. The criminal justice system personnel know that once the law has been broken, someone is to be held responsible. Therefore, it would be foolish for one to think that a crime offender may escape prosecution by assuming that his criminal act will go undetected.

When committing a criminal act, some people try to destroy evidence at the scene and think that they will escape prosecution. However, they fail to understand that other than evidence, there are other factors that can link them to the crime and lead to their arrest and conviction. When investigating a crime, law enforcement officers and personnel do not only search for evidence, but they go beyond that. They also look for links, connections, and motives, anything that might have something to do with the crime. They search for anything that can link a suspect to the crime and anything that may lead to an arrest. Therefore, it would be foolish for anyone to assume that destroying crime evidence will make a criminal act go undetected and escape prosecution. Every intentional criminal act is subject to prosecution. I believe that we are all to think like that.

The capability and the ability to commit crime are within ourselves.

If we are able to prevent every single crime, then the criminal justice system will no longer be necessary and there will not be any criminal offenders. Even when the criminal justice system and law enforcement personnel are doing the best they can to prevent crime, it has been proven that every single crime cannot be prevented. Crime is investigated after it has been committed. The ability to commit crime is within ourselves and we are all capable of violating the criminal law. Unless somebody can control someone else's ideas, thoughts, emotions, capabilities, and abilities to act and react, there is little we can do to prematurely prevent a crime from being committed.

When someone is about to commit a criminal act, there could be many people around him including law enforcement personnel, but if no one knows exactly and precisely what he is thinking and is about to do, there is little they can do to stop or prevent that person from committing the crime.

Law enforcement and the criminal justice system personnel have been doing all they can to fight crime. While they have had some success, it does not account for every single crime. Law enforcement and the criminal justice system personnel have been proven to not be able to prematurely fight all crime successfully because offenders continue to successfully show their ability and capability to commit criminal acts. It is a battle between the law enforcement and the criminal justice system personnel to fight crime and prosecute offenders of criminal acts and those who continue to break the criminal law.

We are all capable of breaking the criminal law.

The battle will continue unless people stop violating the criminal law. I do know for sure that the criminal justice system personnel will not give up on prosecuting those who commit crime. Those who have been victims of a crime know and understand the need of the law enforcement personnel and the criminal justice system for justice. It is scary to know that despite the great effort and the great job of the criminal justice system personnel and some of their success of prosecuting crime offenders, that that will not stop or prevent every single crime from happening and that we can all be victims of criminal acts at any time.

The fact is that the law enforcement and the criminal justice system personnel cannot fight all crime by themselves and cannot prevent all crime from happening. They need *everyone's* help. One of the best ways to fight crime is for every single one of us to stop violating the criminal law. They need our help to not commit unlawful acts ourselves and to stop and prevent others from committing crime that we are aware of. If nobody violates the criminal law, then the world would become crime free. In this case, the law enforcement and the criminal justice system personnel would no longer be needed to fight crime and to prosecute their offenders because there would have been no crime committed. While the criminal justice system is doing all it can to protect and serve us, we also need to help it by not violating the criminal law ourselves, by doing everything with justice, and acting accordingly. While the criminal justice system may not be able to make the world a crime free place, we do have that ability ourselves.

Some individuals continue to show their ability to violate the criminal law despite the great effort of the criminal justice system on fighting crime and prosecuting those responsible.

One of the ways we can show our help is to not violate the criminal law ourselves. The criminal justice system is doing its best and does not wish to prosecute anyone, but unless people stop committing crime, the system will always have a reason and a cause to prosecute those who do. Law enforcement and the criminal justice system study crime, yet they do not have total access to prevent all of them. In some cases, the best they can do is to wish that crime does not happen, but if and/or when it does, they need to prosecute those responsible.

Every crime involves a different location, different witnesses, different evidence, and different times. Even when a crime occurred in the same region and was committed by two different individuals, the two cases will differ from each other. Therefore, every crime is somehow different from each other. If two individuals are arrested under the same charge at two different locations, the charges will remain the same, but the two similar cases will be different.

Law enforcement and the criminal justice system are always faced with similar cases, but they always differ from every other with different evidence, different locations, and different witnesses. Those facts are not always the same in every criminal case. They can study crime offenders and learn from them and their experience, but they cannot always be sure of the kind of evidence every criminal case will produce and provide. They cannot be certain of all the kinds of evidence that will be found or be exactly sure how the crime will be committed second-by-second.

The battle will continue in between the criminal justice system to prosecute those who violate the criminal law and offenders who continue to commit unlawful acts unless we all show respect for the criminal law and act accordingly.

Therefore, the study of crime can be helpful for prosecution, but can sometimes do too little on to prevent it from happening. The study and prosecution of crime cannot successfully prevent every single crime from occurring, but can have some great success on some. Law enforcement personnel continue to study and investigate crime and learn about it every day and the criminal justice system continues to prosecute those who violate the criminal law, yet crime continues to happen.

It is a great concern to us and sometimes it can endanger our lives. One of the reasons law enforcement personnel cannot successfully prevent every single crime from happening is because they cannot control everyone's ability and capability to do so. Moreover, until they can do that, I believe that some people will continue to commit criminal acts.

Everyone who violates the criminal law has different reasons and motives of why he did so and sometimes there is no reason at all. Those reasons and motives must sometimes be known prior to the violation of the law by someone else to somehow be able to help, stop, and prevent the perpetrator from committing the criminal act. In some cases, law enforcement personnel get to know about the motives of a crime after it has been committed. Perhaps if they did know about the motives before the occurrence of the crime, they may have been able to prevent it. It is very difficult for anybody to just look at someone else and be able to tell that he is about to commit a crime.

One of the best ways to fight crime is for every single one of us not to violate the criminal law ourselves.

That is one of the problems that law enforcement personnel are faced with. They cannot just look at someone and be able to tell that that person is about to break the criminal law and the motives why. One other problem is while law enforcement personnel are day-by-day looking for better ways to fight crime, some individuals are scanning through new ways of breaking the criminal law. I believe that sometimes law enforcement personnel wish that the human behavior were like a computer hooked up to a keyboard where they can control it and program it to not be able to violate the criminal law. I believe that sometimes some of the law enforcement personnel hate being disturbed in their donut and coffee break by a call to be dispatched to a crime location. We all need to help the law enforcement personnel on their fight against crime and one of the best things we can do is to not violate the criminal law ourselves. Some of those who commit criminal acts give excuses of why they have violated the criminal law, but it is better not to break the criminal law in the first place, so that no one will have to find an excuse of why we have done so.

The fact is that sometimes people commit crime for a variety of reasons and sometimes that goes beyond our imagination. Sometimes, when imagining about why somebody commits a crime, his or her real motive would have been our last to consider. Even when someone is being punished for a crime they have committed, they can never explain why they have done so. They take their secret to their grave and leave the world wondering why.

While the criminal justice system may not be able to make the world a crime-free place, we do have that ability and that capability.

A lot has been done to give a solution to crime: educate crime offenders, train them, improve opportunities, and deprive them of some legal rights, yet some people continue to break the criminal law because they have the ability and the capability to do so. Unless every single one of us can be deprived of the ability and the capability to violate the criminal law, some people will continue to commit criminal acts. Sometimes, people commit crimes by acting on their own free will while sometimes they do so because they have been put under pressure and have been threatened by someone else to do so. Some others feel the necessity of doing so for whatever reason their motive might be. While some may not commit certain crimes themselves, they use others to do so for them.

There are a variety of reasons why people commit crime. Each crime has its own reason and motive of why it happens. It could be anything such as jealousy, revenge, and more. When it comes to breaking the criminal law, they find it very difficult to fight their intention of doing so. They try to convince themselves that they should not be violated and that there could be consequences for doing so. In some cases, even when someone thinks of the consequences of violating the criminal law before they do so, that does not seem to have an impact on them and they commit the crime anyway. While that is sometimes the case, it is not always. Haven't you ever witnessed, seen on TV, or heard of some people, when given an order by a law enforcement personnel, that they deliberately refuse to do so even when they know that such behavior may result in them violating the criminal law?

Each crime differs significantly from others.

This explains that sometimes, under certain circumstances, some will deliberately break the criminal law, regardless of the tough consequences and the knowledge of them. Such behavior motivates some people to break the criminal law. They keep on challenging the criminal justice system to be tough on them, regardless of how much sympathy the criminal justice system personnel may have for them. I can assure you that the battle will continue between the criminal justice system and those who continue to have no respect and no regard for the criminal law.

While the criminal justice system cannot prevent every single crime from happening, it is doing a great job of making sure that those who commit criminal acts be prosecuted. I say that carefully because if it was not for the law enforcement and the criminal justice system personnel prosecuting and providing consequences for those who violate the criminal law, how do you think committing crime would have been? And how about after they would have occurred?

Experts have been studying crime and their offenders for years. Law enforcement personnel deal with crime offenders day-by-day and even psychologists cannot help with the prevention of all crime. An expert can study and interrogate a crime offender right now, but may not precisely be able to tell if that person will break the criminal law again years later considering. Circumstances that are to happen years later can be substantiated that no one may be able to tell exactly how, when, and where it will happen. On almost every issue, we can assume, presume, and predict, but there may always be room left for circumstances and coincidences. Sometimes, when experts suspect and believe that somebody is likely to break the criminal law, they cannot precisely tell the time, the location, and how he will do so.

I believe that if any one of us had the power to make the world a crime-free place, then it probably would have been.

Those facts and information are crucial to law enforcement personnel to help and prevent anyone from committing a crime. Expert criminal studies are lacking the precise location, time, and evidence to always be able to tell accurately when and how someone will break the criminal law. There are so many experts out there studying crime, why it happened, and how to help prevent them from happening prematurely. While they have had some success, it is not always a total complete success on all crimes. No matter where you live in the world, crime continues to present itself every day.

I have read reports of certain regions of the world where they had a low crime rate. However, low crime rates tell you that crime does happen in those regions and they are not crime-free. No matter how much explanation we have been given about crime, what best to do to prevent them, regardless of the great effort of the law enforcement personnel, the toughness of the criminal justice system on those who commit unlawful acts, and despite the ongoing crime experts' studies and findings, people continue to violate the criminal law. One of the reasons is because we all have the ability and the capability to violate the criminal law and sometimes, nobody else can control our ability or capability to do so except ourselves. We all have the ability and the capability to do so, regardless of what the criminal law says, stands for, and is against because some people do commit criminal acts anyway, even when they know their acts will break the criminal law in the first place. The criminal law itself, despite of what it states, cannot stop some people from violating it. We all have a great job to do when it comes to helping with the prevention of crime. We all need to have respect for the criminal law and to not violate it. We all need to act responsibly and think about what we want to do before we do it and avoid doing what can lead to the violation of the criminal law. We need to think about the consequences of committing criminal acts and to always act accordingly.

The study and prosecution of crime cannot successfully prevent every single crime, but can have some great success on some.

We all need to not behave criminally, have respect for the criminal law, and act accordingly, and that can help with the prevention of crime. If nobody commits criminal acts, then the criminal law will not be violated. Every time that somebody becomes a victim of a crime, it means that someone had violated the criminal law. We all need to act responsibly so that no one becomes a victim of another's crime and to do the best we can to make the world a crime-free place. Together, we can do it. I believe that if we are all committed to it, we can make it happen. You can then call it a miracle. It will be a great miracle to the benefit of all of us and our Father above. God will be very proud of us.

We can make sure that no criminal law is ever broken again and we can help do that by not, first of all, violating it ourselves. The ability, the capability, and motives to break the criminal law are within our control and ourselves. We do not automatically break the criminal law, but we usually choose to do so. By doing so, it will cause others to become victims of our criminal acts. No one should do that to others because I believe that none of us would like to become a victim of others' criminal and irresponsible acts. Unless we are determined not to break the criminal law, there is too little the law enforcement or the criminal justice system personnel can do to help prevent every single crime because they do not have full and total control over every single person's ability and capability to break the criminal law and motives that can lead to do so. Despite their great job and efforts, I believe that they cannot fight the battle against crime by themselves and they need every single person's help and cooperation in their fight against crime and to prevent it. When we help the law enforcement and the criminal justice system personnel in their battle against crime, we also help others and ourselves from becoming victims of criminal acts. And for that, we will be very grateful whether or not a single thanks was said to us for our great effort. We all have a job to do, and let's always act lawfully and responsibly and precisely to others.

We must continue to thank the law enforcement and the criminal justice system personnel for all their great effort and services. And also to continue to support and help them to always be successful on the difficult job they have to do day-by-day and with the prevention of criminal acts. They continue to put their lives on the line every day to protect ours. Let's give them credit for that and let them know that we appreciate them because they truly deserve it.

I myself personally thank them and congratulate them. Salute!

Chapter 2

The System

One of the reasons law enforcement and the criminal justice system personnel cannot prevent every single crime from happening is because they cannot control everyone's ability and capability to violate the criminal law.

-Roldimy Montinar

The fact that some people continue to violate the criminal law, the criminal justice system has to keep on prosecuting those who do. Nevertheless, I must carefully say that the way the criminal justice system prosecutes criminal act offenders is not always at its best. Let me get something straight, from a psychological point, I believe that there is no such thing as a non-criminal. Let's be realistic. I'm not accusing anyone nor pointing fingers at anybody; that's not the purpose of this book. I believe that there is no one who is at least 21 years of age who has not at least once violated the criminal law.

Not every single one who violated the criminal law is prosecuted. One can argue that we have all broken the criminal law whether there was prosecution or not. If everyone is prosecuted for every single time they break the criminal law, then you surely know that there would not have been enough room in jail to put the offenders. The law enforcement and the criminal justice system personnel know that.

Sometimes, the criminal justice system personnel choose and pick whom to prosecute for breaking the criminal law. If everyone had at least broken the criminal law once, then everyone should have been prosecuted for that purpose. I do not think nor believe that the law allows the criminal justice system personnel to pick and choose just who they want to prosecute. The law is equal to everyone. However, the criminal justice system personnel sometimes use the law to discriminate against whom they choose to prosecute. While it has been said that we have all at least once broken the criminal law, some will argue that law enforcement and the criminal justice system personnel have to be aware of every single crime to be able to fully prosecute all of them.

While it is sometimes the case, it is not always the thought about the consequences of breaking the criminal law that prevent some from doing so.

Law enforcement personnel do not know of every single time the criminal law has been broken and by whom, which makes it difficult for them to prosecute certain crimes that they are not aware of. However, at the same time, in some cases, they have knowledge of certain crimes, but they choose not to prosecute the offender. One can argue that it's wrong because if some are prosecuted for violating the criminal law, then others should not be allowed to just walk away and escape prosecution when they also break the criminal law. I do not believe that the criminal law allows the non-prosecution of anybody who violates it. One can argue that if one should get prosecuted for breaking the criminal law, then all should also be prosecuted for crimes they commit, no exceptions. If the criminal law should allow some who violate it to be prosecuted and some others who also break it not to be prosecuted, then the saying of *the judicial system personnel use the criminal law to discriminate against who they pick and choose to prosecute* is probably true. One can argue that, yes, under certain circumstances and in some cases, the criminal justice system personnel sometimes do pick and choose who to prosecute.

Experts' crime studies are sometimes lacking the precise location, time, and evidence to always be able to tell accurately by whom, how, when, and where the criminal law will be violated.

Some say that there is something wrong with the criminal law. I disagree and believe that it has a lot more to do with those who are in charge of it. The law states what it says and we should all follow it under any circumstances including those who are in charge of it. However, those who are in charge of it sometimes bend it, use it, and apply it in their own way. By doing so, they do not change the content of it; they just misuse it.

One can argue that they do not always use it and apply the criminal law for what it says. Two people may in the same county be charged with the same crime and have the same background. If they are both convicted, their sentences may differ. One may get a stiffer sentence than the other. One may get probation and the other some jail time. If they are tried in the same county for violating the same crime and are covered under the same criminal law, why do they get two different sentences? It tells that even when the law states what it says, sometimes those in charge of it use it in their own way.

Under certain circumstances, some courts allow testimonies to be heard at the sentencing to consider the kind of sentence to apply, but not always. If a court should once hear testimonies at the sentencing to consider whether to lower or stiffen the sentence, that same court should always apply that same rule to his every sentencing case, at least to show fairness. Because the criminal justice system is supposed to act under the criminal law and the criminal law is supposed to be even, it should be the same for every single particular criminal case.

We all have the ability and the capability to violate the criminal law and sometimes nobody else can control our ability and capability to do so but ourselves.

If under certain circumstances, the judicial system should allow witness testimonies at sentencing in a criminal case, then under those same circumstances, witness testimonies should be allowed at sentencing to every particular case of that pattern. ***The criminal law is not to be broken nor bent by anyone and nor should anyone use and apply it in their own way other than what it states.*** Nevertheless, it happens. Those in charge of the law sometimes use it in their own way and pick whom to prosecute and choose whom to give a lighter sentence to. I believe that the criminal law states how the criminal justice system personnel should always apply it, but they do not always go by how the criminal law states itself. Therefore, it is not really the law that is the problem, but it is how those in charge of it choose to use and apply it. Sometimes they will just use it to their own advantage. I believe that is wrong because the criminal law should not be used or applied to anyone's advantage.

When some criminal justice system personnel filed charges against someone accused of committing a criminal act, if they later find out, discover, or become aware that they have the wrong person, they may instead of dropping the charges against that person, offer him a plea deal, at which may sometimes be considered as consent of guilt. I believe that that is wrong because I do not believe that the criminal law allows any criminal justice system personnel to ask anybody to consent to a crime they did not commit. It is simply wrong and I do not think that anyone needs the criminal law to condemn it to acknowledge that.

If nobody commits criminal acts, then the criminal law would not be violated.

It would be reasonable to say that the criminal law should support and allow the non-prosecution of anyone who did not violate it. Under any circumstances, if someone has been wrongly charged with a crime, the criminal charges against him should be dropped, but not ask him to consent to the crime he has been wrongfully charged with and that he did not commit. In the criminal justice system, it happens sometimes, and that is flatly wrong and that should be unlawful. As an act of fairness, nobody would like to be charged, prosecuted, or convicted for a crime they did not commit. I do not believe that anybody would like that to happen to them and it scares some to find out that sometimes it may have been the case to some others. That does not mean that every time that someone is being offered a plea deal that he was wrongly charged. What I am saying is that, sometimes, and under certain circumstances, some of the criminal justice system personnel may charge the wrong person with a crime, but when they become aware that they have the wrong person, they should drop the charges. One can argue that sometimes they do not do that; they would rather offer a plea deal, which is like asking the wrongfully charged person to consent to the crime. In some cases, if the person they wrongfully charged rejects the plea deal, they may not drop the criminal charges against him, but will try to proceed to trial. If the case is not dismissed and does proceed to trial, they know for a fact that they are prosecuting the wrong person, but they will bend the criminal law, use it in their own way, and will do everything within their power to get that wrong person convicted. Will anyone dare call that justice? That has been proven many times in many criminal cases. They get the wrong person convicted and serving time for a crime they never committed, but when evidence is presented at the appeal, they are released. One can argue that, unfortunately, not all who are wrongly convicted won an appeal.

With few exceptions, from a psychological point, there are not a lot of person on Earth at least 21 years of age who may not have at least once violated the criminal law.

That should tell you what some in charge of the criminal law may do and how far they may go to get a conviction. When they charge someone with a crime and later find out they have the wrong person, they may not want to drop the criminal charges for many reasons such as:

- It may have an impact on the way they choose to charge other people

- It may sometimes leave the public with doubt and wondering the next time they charge someone else with a similar charge

- The performance of their job can be unfairly and wrongly questioned by anyone about prior and future criminal cases

- The performance of the job, his or her ability and capability to do the job right can be criticized by anyone

- Lawsuits

- The public's loss of confidence in them

- Under certain circumstances, it can and may be used against them

- It may always leave room for doubt and for some to speculate

- They may feel shame

- And some other factors

Every case will have its own speculations and circumstances. Regardless, nobody should be prosecuted for a crime they did not commit. The criminal justice system personnel wants everyone who violates the criminal law to be held responsible for their criminal act, just as they themselves should accept responsibility for their own action. No excuses, no exceptions.

If they become aware that they have the wrong person, they should drop the charges, regardless. I say regardless because I believe that nobody should be held accountable for someone else's unlawful act. I am not sure if it is unlawful to prosecute someone for a crime they did not commit, but I believe that the law does not state for anyone to be prosecuted for a crime they did not commit. Anyone who prosecutes someone for a crime he did not commit, I believe, bends the criminal law. And that is an act of injustice. Anybody who is ever prosecuted for a crime they did not commit is a victim of injustice and a victim of the misuse of the criminal law. The criminal law is to give justice to all. I strongly believe that. There is justice for those who are victims of unlawful acts and consequences for those who break the criminal law. One of the purposes of the criminal law is to give justice, but not to make anyone become a victim of its misuse.

Some of the criminal justice system personnel sometimes pick and choose whom to prosecute who break the criminal law.

It is my understanding that crime happens day-by-day and that is why we have law enforcement and the criminal justice system personnel, but let's go after the right person. Let's not make someone else pay the consequences for what somebody else did. If someone is charged with a crime and it is later proven that he did not commit it, do not then try to build an unfit case against him so that he can get prosecuted anyway, but drop the criminal charges against him. That's what the law is about: *justice for all.* Don't use the law to do injustice to others. Let's not just prosecute people because we want to and let's not use the criminal law for our advantage, but only for what it states. If the criminal law is used and applied as it states, then no one should ever be prosecuted and convicted for a crime they did not commit. We all need to not violate or bend the law under any circumstances and for whatever reason. We all have the ability and the capability to go by what the criminal law says and we do have the control over doing what is according to it. Whoever breaks the criminal law should be prosecuted. Whoever did not violate the criminal law should not get prosecuted. We all can always use the criminal law to do what is right, apply it with justice, and to always act and behave accordingly. Nobody should be a victim of the misuse of the criminal law because I believe that that is not what the criminal law is intended for. Unfortunately, it does happen and now is the time to always use it for what it stands for: *justice for all.*

Some of the criminal justice system personnel sometimes use the criminal law to discriminate against whom they pick and choose to prosecute.

It has been said before; we have all at least once violated the criminal law. Let's take this scenario for example. Six neighbors went to a bar and got drunk. Neighbor 1 got in a car, drove, and got home safe. Neighbor 2 got pulled over by law enforcement personnel and was arrested for DUI. She was prosecuted and was found guilty by a jury and was sentenced. Neighbor 3 was detected by law enforcement personnel and was taken into custody. She was prosecuted and was found not guilty by a jury. Neighbor 4 was stopped by law enforcement personnel and was taken to jail. She was charged with DUI, but the charges against her were dropped. Neighbor 5 was pulled over and was taken into custody. She was prosecuted and the court dismissed her case. Neighbor 6 was detected by law enforcement personnel, but she did not get arrested because the officer knew her and gave her a break, and had her take a taxi home.

I see something seriously wrong with this pattern. All six neighbors broke the same criminal law and they were all covered under the same criminal law, but the outcome of their case differs from each other. Only Neighbor 2 was convicted for violating the criminal law. One can argue that there is something terribly wrong with the system. Only Neighbor 2 suffers the consequences and was held responsible for violating the criminal law and at the same time, they let the other five neighbors walk away free. One can argue that even when Neighbor 3 was found not guilty by a jury and walked away free and was not held responsible for violating the criminal law, the system discriminated against her for prosecuting her and not prosecuting Neighbor 1 for breaking the same criminal law. Let me be clear when I say discriminate. I'm talking about the unequal use of the same criminal law in different contrary ways. The fact that all six violated the same criminal law and the fact that the criminal law states the same in all six cases, the outcome of all six should have been the same and they all should have gone through the same process.

If one should be prosecuted for violating the criminal law, then all who commit criminal acts should also be prosecuted for breaking the criminal law, no exceptions.

According to the outcome of all six cases, Neighbor 2 can argue that the system was not being fair to her, not in a sense that she did not commit the criminal act, but for the fact that she was the only one to be convicted. One factor to consider is that in all criminal cases, while the process may be the same in a specific county, the locations, the witnesses, and the evidence will be different. Some criminal cases have stronger evidence than others do. The more evidence the criminal justice system has against you, the better chance it has on getting you convicted. In addition, the criminal law does allow guilt to be determined in some cases and where applicable by a jury. Therefore, while the criminal law states what it says and is to be equal to every single one, the judicial process from the time someone is arrested may differ in every single criminal case. The process might be the same or similar, but the pleadings, motions, witnesses, locations, evidence, and other crucial factors relevant to the case may differ in every single criminal case. Sometimes, in some places, the law does allow those proceedings (where allowed) including the defendant's rights to a fair trial and his innocence and the prosecutions rights to prove the defendant's guilt. (Be aware that the law differs significantly from place to place.)

One can argue that the differences in all six cases above may have been differed because of their different proceedings and process. However, there is no question and no doubt that all six of them violated the criminal law. The process and the proceedings might differ from each other, but there are no difference in all six of them violating the same criminal law and no room left to argue the reality of what they all did. The difference in the process and proceedings of all six cases does not mean that all six neighbors did not truly break the criminal law. Neighbor 1 was not detected by any law enforcement personnel, so she was not arrested even when she violated the criminal law by driving drunk and when the criminal law itself states that it is a criminal act to do so. The fact that she was not detected was that there was probably no evidence to be used against her and even if witnesses would have come forward to report the criminal act, there was too little the criminal justice system could have done to prosecute her because she was not detected while driving drunk.

I do not believe that the criminal law allows the non-prosecution of anyone who violates the criminal law.

Therefore, she did not have to deal with the criminal justice system and she did not have to go through any criminal proceedings. Neighbors 2, 3, 4, 5, and 6 were all detected, but their proceedings differed from each other. The differences may have been reflected in the proceedings of the criminal justice system where the criminal law allowed (where allowed) evidence, witnesses to be presented on both sides, and for each side to argue their case to the result they wanted. While the criminal law may state that everyone who commits a criminal act should be prosecuted, it does not mean that the violation of the law is an automatic guilt; it will have to be proven. You have to go through the criminal justice system process and proceedings where your guilt will be determined. Everyone is presumed innocent until found guilty when charged with a criminal act. The violation of the criminal law does not lawfully mean that you are guilty and/or automatically guilty of the crime. It is not when you break a law that states your guilt, it is the process and proceedings where witnesses are being heard and evidence is being presented that make that determination. The criminal law may state that every single one who breaks the criminal law should be prosecuted and there are also rules of evidence, but the criminal law itself does not know exactly who will break the criminal law, or how, where, when, and what evidence will be presented in every single criminal case and who the witnesses will be. Not knowing those facts prior to anyone breaking the criminal law, the criminal law could not arrange itself in any way to disadvantage some and advantage some others who break the same criminal law.

The criminal justice system personnel do not always apply the criminal law for what it states.

Not knowing those crucial facts prior to anyone committing a crime, the criminal law could not arrange itself to discriminate itself against anyone by the differences in the outcome of every single particular criminal case. The criminal law is not flexible in a sense that you can bend it one way for one case and another way for another case. It should not be used or applied that way. Furthermore, the law states what it says, but it is the criminal justice system's process and proceedings that everyone accused of violating the criminal law will go through that determine your guilt. The determination of anyone's guilt has a lot more to do with the process and proceedings that every single criminal case goes through than what the criminal law itself says. If anyone intentionally violates the criminal law, doesn't that mean that they are guilty of the crime? Yes and no. From a psychological point, yes, because the offender knows and understands that he broke the criminal law. He does not need anybody else to judge and question him for him to acknowledge the reality of his criminal act. From a legal definition term, no. He will have to be found guilty or convicted, so he will have to be prosecuted and his guilt will have to be proven.

The intentional violation of the criminal law by anyone does not mean an automatic guilt. When charged with a crime, everyone is presumed innocent until found guilty or convicted whether they committed the crime or not. From a legal standpoint, nobody is a criminal because they simply violated the criminal law. They have to be convicted of a criminal act to be considered a criminal. Some people break the criminal law all the time and they will continue to do so every day around the world, but unless they are detected, are prosecuted, and convicted, they are not criminals. (That is from a legal definition term.)

Some others who violate the criminal law, get prosecuted, and convicted are complaining and arguing that if they are considered criminals for breaking the criminal law, then everyone else who violated the criminal law is also a criminal whether they were convicted or not. Their arguments are based on a psychological point. The fact is not everyone who violated the criminal law will be detected, prosecuted, and convicted. The criminal law does not automatically nor immediately apply itself nor act personally against anyone by the same time they break it. That right there leaves room for speculation on every single criminal case.

If in a criminal case, a court should rule for or against under certain circumstances, then that same court should always apply the same strategies under the same circumstances in every other particular criminal case of that pattern.

Everyone who breaks the criminal law would have been detected and prosecuted only if the execution of the criminal law was within ourselves, where every time we violated the criminal law, it sent a signal that automatically took action against us. However, for as long as the execution of the law is conducted by law enforcement and the criminal judicial system personnel, crime will continue to go undetected. Some individuals will continue to be prosecuted for a crime they did not commit, some people will continue to escape prosecution and conviction for their criminal acts, and some of the criminal justice system personnel may continue to pick and choose who to prosecute or not.

The criminal law states what it says, but the law enforcement and the criminal justice system personnel execute it. Therefore, bad judgment will remain and may sometimes lead to unlawful prosecution or wrongful conviction. At jury's trial, it is the jurors' judgment that determines the defendant's guilt or innocence. When faced with a jury trial, it is not really if you did commit the crime or not that will determine your guilt, but it is up to the jury's belief. Do they believe you are innocent or guilty? In a jury trial, whether you committed the crime you are being prosecuted for may not be relevant to the determination of your guilt, but only what the jury believes. The jury is to make the determination. Sometimes they may find someone guilty when they are truly innocent and they may get someone acquitted when they are really guilty.

Everyone who has faced a jury trial should know that very well and criminal defense trial lawyers understand that as well. So many have been found guilty by a jury and were sentenced to jail for a crime they did not commit and they later won an appeal. Some people might be serving time right now for a crime they may not have truly committed, but the jury believed they did and got them convicted. Some of them may, perhaps, win an appeal and some would not, and some may have to spend the rest of their life in jail.

We must continue to thank the law enforcement and the criminal justice system personnel for all their great effort and services. And also to continue to support and help them to always be successful on the difficult job they have to do day-by-day and with the prevention of criminal acts. They continue to put their lives on the line every day to protect ours. Let's give them credit for that and let them know that we appreciate them because they truly deserve it.

I myself personally thank them and congratulate them. Salute!

Chapter 3

Jury

The criminal law is not to be used to anyone's advantage but as it states.

-Roldimy Montinar

In a jury trial, your guilt or innocence may be determined by the juror's good or bad judgment. Some who really commit a crime are acquitted by a jury and walk away free. In some places, the criminal law does allow jury trial and allows jurors to determine the defendants' guilt or innocence. The criminal law (where applicable) allows the jury to determine a defendant's guilt or innocence by their judgment and belief, but the criminal law does not directly advise the jurors when or where to use their good or bad judgment, nor in which particular criminal case to apply them. The criminal law has no control over the juror's good or bad judgment and belief, nor does the criminal law know when, how, or where they will use them.

A jury's verdict in every single criminal case is either fair justice or injustice. If a jury returns a guilty verdict in a case where the defendant really did commit the crime, then it is fair justice. If a jury returns a guilty verdict in a case where the defendant is truly innocent, it is injustice, from a psychological point. None of us would like to become a victim of injustice including jurors. One can argue that the fact that the jurors can sometimes use their bad judgment, every time they return a guilty verdict and before sentencing, that the defense should have been able to question them of why they did so. Perhaps, maybe, there can be some evidence that the defense can present or redirect to the jurors or other witnesses. That may be able to tell the jurors that they have used their bad judgment. However, at the same time, prosecutors may disagree with such process and proceedings because they want conviction and that is what they usually push for in a criminal case.

What is the purpose of prosecuting a suspect? Isn't it for the crime the criminal justice system personnel believed they committed? Is the purpose of prosecution to get people convicted whether they are innocent or not? Why push for conviction when it has been proven that the defendant is innocent of the crime being charged with and being prosecuted for? Should prosecutors have any problem at all with the process and proceedings to prove a defendant's innocence? We are all to ask ourselves those questions and find the best answers to them.

The criminal law does not state for anyone to be prosecuted for a crime they did not commit.

One of the jurors' primary jobs is to witness the trial and to make their determination according to evidences presented, testimonies heard from witnesses, and other crucial factors allowed by the criminal law. Sometimes, and in some cases, a juror can make his determination of guilt or innocence before the trial even gets started. On the other hand, a juror may choose to support the prosecution's weak evidence over the defense's stronger one just to determine the guilt of a defendant. A jury may also choose to undermine the prosecution's stronger evidence over the defense's weaker one just to determine a defendant's innocence.

Just like in a criminal trial, each side presents evidence to support their claim and do all they can to undermine the other side's evidence. Where jurors are selected for a criminal jury trial, they were not witnesses of the crime that the defendant is accused of. Therefore, they do not know for sure if the defendant is truly guilty or innocent, but they are to make that determination during trial according to testimonies heard from witnesses and evidence presented and other crucial factors. The fact is, after the verdict, if they reach one, some of the jurors may come out of the court wondering just like anybody else if the defendant is truly guilty or innocent. That can be a burden and have them wondering for the rest of their life. They can only hope that their verdict was fair. The fact is that the verdict is based on the process and the proceedings of the trial, but they can never be certain of what really happened. Moreover, they may never get to know or find out. Therefore, questioning the fairness of their verdict is something they may have to live with for the rest of their life. This may not be an easy task or experience.

- False and forged evidence

- False testimonies

- Witnesses lying on the stand

- The defense and prosecution inability, unable to find and present crucial evidence

- Jurors not entirely involved in the trial

- Jurors taking and supporting side

- Jurors making determinations prior to the trial

- Jurors not have been a witness of the crime

- People being wrongly charged and unlawfully prosecuted

All these and others may have an impact on the outcome of a jury verdict.

Anyone who is prosecuted for a crime they did not commit is a victim of injustice.

Can you imagine what a defendant feels like when he has to hear a witness lying about him on the stand and there is nothing he can say at that time to question the witness and prove that he is not telling the truth? What about when a witness is lying on the stand and most of the people in the courtroom know it, but there is no way to prove that he is not telling the truth?

In some cases, only the person who's accused of committing the crime, the victim of the criminal acts, and witnesses truly know if the accused person is innocent or not. Therefore, a jury's determination can be just guessing. Sometimes, even the law enforcement and the criminal justice system personnel who are prosecuting the defendant and even the defendant's lawyer who is defending him do not really know if he is guilty or innocent. However, they can always assume and speculate. Sometimes, if a juror wants to get a defendant convicted or acquitted, no matter what has been proven at trial, it may not change his mind, but he is more likely to take note of evidence and testimonies that support his intention. One can argue that the fact that the jurors are not usually lawyers and do not know the criminal law and the rules of evidence may have a serious impact in their determination. For example: if someone was a victim of a burglary and later becomes a juror in a burglary criminal case, regardless of what was proven at trial, he may make his determination prior to the trial based on the fact that he himself was a victim of a crime. However, what happens to him is not relevant to the case he was a juror of; it is wrong for that juror to do so. The court, however, was not aware of the juror's wrongful act; otherwise, the court may not have allowed it and may have dismissed that juror. The court must be aware of the juror's wrongful act relevant to a criminal case to excuse him from it. Unfortunately, that is not always the case.

One of the purposes of the criminal law is to give justice, but not make anyone become a victim of injustice by its misuse and misapply.

Many of us will continue to be subjected to the daily circumstances of the criminal law. When jurors are to make their determination and before they return a verdict, they must acknowledge that they were not witnesses of the crime the defendant is accused of and is on trial for and they should decide wisely, fairly, and carefully. They must consider the fact that their verdict can get the defendant acquitted for a crime he did commit or get him convicted for a crime he is truly innocent of. They must always use their good faith for fair justice to all, no exceptions.

Not everybody who violates the criminal law is detected. Even the jurors, law enforcement, and the criminal justice system personnel may sometimes commit a crime that goes undetected and they may never be prosecuted for them. Jurors may be selected to make determinations on criminal cases alleging crime they have themselves committed, but went undetected. Some of the criminal justice system and law enforcement personnel take advantage of the system to prosecute some people whether they have a good case against them or not. They offer them plea deals or face trials. Ask a defendant to consent to a crime that the prosecution knows that they will not be able to prove and that they never had a case to start up with in the first place. They know at jury trial, the defendant's guilt will not be determined by whether they are guilty of the crime being charged with, but by the jurors' belief and judgment. They do know that in some cases, jurors are more likely to return a verdict in their favor even when they have not really proven their case.

If the criminal law is applied and used as it states, then no one should ever be prosecuted for a crime he did not commit.

It should not be like that. It is wrong and is pure injustice. Anybody who is prosecuted for a crime he did not commit and is convicted for it is a victim of injustice. It is contrary to what the criminal law states and is intended for. Let's no longer disregard what the criminal law says or bend it to anyone's advantage to do injustice to others. Let's no longer bend the criminal law, make it flexible for our own use, but use and apply it only for what it states. We all may have at least once become to admire what we once hated. Someone who is a victim of a crime may more likely be outraged and ask that anyone responsible to be prosecuted to the fullest extent of the criminal law and to be given the maximum sentence allowed by the criminal law. They may even want to go beyond the criminal law and demand that that person be given a sentence stiffer than what the criminal law states. However, if that same victim becomes accused of violating the criminal law, he may most likely be outspoken against the criminal justice system and ask for his non-prosecution. If convicted, he may demand that he be given the lightest sentence possible.

One of the prosecutor's jobs is to prosecute criminal cases. They go against the defense and seek conviction. However, a prosecutor who is accused of a crime may most likely join the defense, go and speak against what he used to do, screaming for his non-prosecution, ask that he not be charged, and demand the dismissal of his case. If convicted, he may file an appeal, regardless of how guilty he knows he is of the crime he is being charged with.

Criminal defense lawyers go against prosecutors and do everything to get their clients set free. However, if they become a victim of a crime, they will themselves ask that whoever is responsible to be charged, prosecuted, and get convicted.

Breaking a criminal law may not assure your guilt at trial.

Circumstances sometimes allow and permit us to go against what we once asked for. A crime's victim asks for prosecution, conviction, and sentencing. Crime offenders ask for dismissal of their case. Some defendants, even when they know that they are guilty of the crime they are being charged with, will most likely try to fight it. They will tell you, "Why give up without a fight?" They think, perhaps a fight might set them free. Some prosecutors, even when they know that the case they are prosecuting is false, may proceed anyway with hope that the jury may support them.

The law states what it says, but it does not execute itself nor does it give justice automatically. The criminal justice system personnel execute, use, and apply it to give justice. Sometimes, they may purposely pretend to use the criminal law to wrongly prosecute some people by knowingly misusing it and pretending to apply it to do injustice by misapplying it. They sometimes use the criminal law however they want and they get the advantage of the criminal law itself not being able to personally tell them that it is not to be used flexibly in conflicting ways, but only one way, for what it states. They sometimes apply the criminal law any way they want and sometimes in ways that the criminal law itself may state that it is a violation. They get the advantage of the criminal law not being able to personally rebut them. The worst is, sometimes they refer to the criminal when they use and apply it against what it states to do injustice. There can be some serious consequences when the system wrongfully prosecutes a person for a crime he did not commit.

When a town is hit by a serious crime and it is being reported on TV, radio, and newspapers, the offender is at large. In some cases, law enforcement and the criminal justice system personnel are more likely to prosecute any unfortunate one who matches their profile that they can put their hands on to calm people down, to make them feel safe again, to send a signal that no crime goes unpunished in this town, to restore people's faith in the system, to stop people from worrying. However, everyone's worst nightmare is that the real crime offender is out there and anybody can become his next victim. He may continue to commit crime until he finally is caught.

The criminal law states what it says, but it is the criminal justice system's process and proceedings that determine a defendant's guilt.

Chances are that not all of us who are engaged with the criminal law will be treated fairly and equally. Prosecutors may continue to prosecute weak criminal cases when they know that they should not have. They may also continue to drop charges against defendants they have a good case against and that they know that that person should have been prosecuted to the fullest extent of the law.

The way they treat the criminal law tells us that the execution of the criminal law is not always at its best. The fact that the criminal law goes through ever-changing statutes, tells us that there is always room for change.

When faced with the criminal law, arguments that make perfect sense from a psychological point may not be relevant unless supported by the criminal law. When faced with a criminal charge, you cannot go to court and simply make an argument based from a psychological point and expect it to help you with your case. Argument based from a psychological point can be used and be taken under consideration to make changes to the criminal law when the time comes to do so. You can pray, ask, and demand the criminal justice personnel to always use the law for what it states, but that can do too little to help with the use of it against what it says.

The criminal justice system can offer the ultimate sentence to whoever violates the criminal law, but that can do too little to help with crime. One can argue that the use of a jury trial to determine a defendant's guilt or innocence is not at all its best. If you have a trial and have three different sets of jury witnessing the same trial away from each other and each set deliberating separately from each other, chances are that each one of them may come with a different verdict. Jurors' vote for a verdict is usually split up. In a set of 12, you may have: 10-2, 9-3, 8-4, 7-5, or 6-6 votes.

From a psychological point, everyone who violates the criminal law is a criminal, but legally, you are a criminal until you are convicted of a criminal act.

The side that has the most votes wins the verdict for determination. If most of them vote for a guilty verdict, then the verdict may most likely be guilty. If less of them vote for a guilty verdict, then the verdict may most likely be not guilty. If all witness the same trial and they do not see it the same way, why vote differently? Why do their votes differ if they witness the same trial and are to determine a defendant's freedom or not? That tells whoever is faced with a criminal jury trial is to be acquitted or found guilty depending on:

- Who the jurors are
- How differently they vote
- How differently they participate in the trial
- How different they are
- How differently they see the evidences
- How differently they consider the testimonies heard
- How fair or unfair they are
- How differently they define justice and injustice
- How different their instincts are
- How different their commonsense is
- How different their beliefs are
- How different their thoughts and ideas are
- How different their good and bad judgment is
- How differently they guess on issues
- How differently they consider and see issues
- How different their background is
- How differently they define right and wrong
- How different is their ability or inability to use good faith
- How different are their capability or incapability to use fair judgment

A good defense lawyer knows that he has to be able to convince the jurors and challenge the prosecution on those issues when necessary. This question could be an issue at a jury criminal trial: *How can a criminal defense lawyer or the prosecution get most of the jurors to decide on their side?* When faced with a jury trial, you are to be judged by those who do not know what really happened, who has no idea if you are guilty or not, and who were not witnesses of the crime. They are to judge you on their belief and sometimes their belief differs from each other. Sometimes, even after they return a verdict, they keep on questioning themselves whether their verdict was fair justice given or served and they may never get to know.

One can argue that the jury trial may sometimes be like a guessing puzzle game. They heard the evidence and seen the evidence of both sides. And each side is rebutting the other side's claim making it very difficult for the jurors to have a clear idea or a better understanding of who's telling the truth. The fact that they were not witnesses of the crime, they are to sometimes guess and turn in a verdict that supports their strongest belief.

In a criminal jury trial, a defendant's guilt or innocence may be determined by the jurors' good or bad judgment.

According to the criminal law, a criminal is a person convicted of a criminal act and most of us consider it that way. One can argue that it is not always when a person is convicted of a crime that he is a criminal.

As we have seen earlier, sometimes people are wrongly prosecuted and convicted for a crime they did not commit. Such conviction is unfair and does not really affirm the defendant's guilt. One can also argue that there are some who have not been convicted of any crime, but they are criminals for the fact that they may have violated the criminal law, but went undetected and were granted an automatic non-prosecution. Some others do get charged, but their criminal case was dismissed or they dropped the charges against them. Case dismissal or non-prosecution does not necessarily confirm innocence. From a psychological point, those who use their commonsense may consider a criminal anyone who violates the criminal law, regardless if he was convicted or not. The criminal law is intended to give justice to all and those in charge of it are supposed to execute it that way. When someone who commits a crime goes undetected or escapes prosecution or conviction, he is likely to commit others. When someone who commits a crime sees someone else get blamed or punished for the crime, he is likely to commit others.

A wrong conviction does not always affirm guilt.

Defendants in criminal cases are more likely to question evidence that proves their stories are untrue even when they know that their stories are twisted. Interrogators will continue to have a hard time questioning people until they can get them to speak for themselves and to tell events as they remember them. People who are not telling the truth with their mouths know in their mind that they are lying, but their minds cannot speak aloud for everybody to hear.

Criminal cases that were not dropped or dismissed prior to trial send a signal to the jury that there is probable cause even when there is not. According to the criminal law, all defendants are presumed innocent until found guilty, but sometimes, prosecutors play it as if some defendants are guilty until proven innocent. Sometimes, even the proof of their innocence may not save them from wrongful prosecution and an unfair verdict.

We all need to appreciate the great job that the law enforcement and the criminal justice system personnel are doing. Honestly. Without their every day efforts, crime would have been more popular and happen more often. Those who are more likely to commit crime would have gotten their freedom to do so whenever they wanted, however they felt, wherever they wished, and created more fear. Many of us would have continuously become victims of crime and with nowhere to go for help. While prosecution may not stop some from violating the criminal law, it does make some others have a second thought about doing so.

We must continue to thank the law enforcement and the criminal justice system personnel for all their great effort and services. And also to continue to support and help them to always be successful on the difficult job they have to do day-by-day and with the prevention of criminal acts. They continue to put their lives on the line every day to protect ours. Let's give them credit for that and let them know that we appreciate them because they truly deserve it.

I myself personally thank them and congratulate them. Salute!

Chapter 4

Representation

A criminal case, wrongful dismissal, or a defendant's wrongful acquaintance does not confirm innocence.

-Roldimy Montinar

These days, a lot of us have dealt, are dealing, and will be dealing with lawyers, whether for legal advice, legal matters, civil and criminal issues, and more. When it comes to legal issues, many of us have to refer to a lawyer. Some may have not dealt with them and are hoping and wishing that they may never have to. However, there is no certain guarantee that it will not happen. Lawyers are getting new clients every day because legal issues matter every single day. Some legal issues may not require the help of a lawyer, but some still consider it as a must. Even lawyers when they are in trouble with the criminal law, hire another lawyer to represent them.

To successfully resolve some legal issues, one may have to hire a lawyer even when his help is not necessary. When you step inside a courthouse, you may witness all kinds of people dealing with lawyers. One of the reasons we may need a lawyer's assistance when it comes to legal issues is because we do not know the law and we are not professionally trained to present or defend cases in the court of law. Even lawyers cannot memorize the whole book of law. They may be able to tell you right away what is lawful or not, but to refer to the exact law statutes that state their claim, they may have to do a little research. While some lawyers may know exactly where to look for a specific law statute, chances are they may not be able to memorize all the law statutes article-by-article, section-by-section. A lawyer may be able to tell you that certain behaviors are unlawful, but referring to the exact law statutes that state they are unlawful acts may require a little opening of the book of law.

In a civil lawsuit, loss is not to be an option, but a possible outcome.

You may not want to represent yourself in court on any legal issue where when you make a claim, accusation, or objection proper to the rule of law and you cannot refer to the exact law statutes that allow you to do that. Nor would you like to be in a situation where you are making true legal argument, but you are unable to tell the court what law statutes that state that the court should rule in your favor. Nor do you want to be in a situation where you have evidence that you would like to present to the court, but you do not know how to do so properly according to the rules of evidence and the rules of law.

You do not want to be in a situation where you want to call witnesses to the stand, examine, or cross-examine them because you cannot do so effectively according to the rules of law, which may reflect many of your asked questions to be followed by, "Objection!"

Some good cases are dismissed or are ruled against all the time for the party's lack of proving their cases and claims effectively and for not being able to follow proper legal procedure according to the rules of law. If someone cannot or does not know how to follow proper legal procedures and wants to represent himself in a legal matter in a court of law where legal process and procedures have to be followed properly, chances are he may risk losing his case even when he had the opportunity to have made the outcome otherwise.

When you have all those above factors and issues at stake, you may be better off getting a lawyer involved to help you. When you have legal issues that are beyond your ability to represent yourself properly and effectively in the court of law, you should always take the help of a lawyer under consideration. Even the best lawyers sometimes lose cases they thought they might win.

If a matter has no legal basis, then it has no legal merit.

Lawyers sometimes take chances on making an argument or speculating on claims that they cannot prove according to the rules of the law hoping they will get away with it. That is not always the case though. Haven't you ever been to court and heard the lawyer's argument? Sound confusing? Well, that's because it is confusing sometimes even for the court and lawyers. Lawyers are trained to make legal arguments according to the rules of law. However, those who are not lawyers are most likely to make commonsense arguments and presume it to be legal. I cannot tell you how many times I have witnessed clients arguing with their lawyers. Many of us confuse "commonsense argument" and "legal argument." Commonsense argument may make sense through understanding, but legal argument has to make sense legally. If an argument does not make sense legally and is not supported by the rules of law, then it is not a legal argument. Legal argument has to be in reference to the rules of law. Therefore, an argument that may make sense through the use of commonsense may not do so legally. An argument that may make perfect sense may not be relevant to the law. If someone who is not a lawyer is to represent himself in a court of law, he is more likely to make commonsense argument where no matter how much he truly thinks he has proven his case and how well he believes he did, he did absolutely nothing or prove anything because there are no rules of law to support his arguments and claims.

Some people have chosen to represent themselves in litigation that they know that the other party had a lawyer representing them. They go to court, make some good commonsense arguments, and do their best. However, what they don't understand is that they did not prove nor disprove anything. The fact is that their arguments had no legal basis and then they sometimes wonder why they lose despite their great effort.

Commonsense may not be relevant to legal issues.

They may also wonder how the other side's lawyer defeated them with such little effort compared to all they have done. In the court of law, an argument of 60 minutes that has no legal basis can be won by an argument of 5 minutes that is supported by the rules of law. It is not how long you can make a successful argument, but how you can do so effectively according to the rules of law and prove your claims accordingly. Even lawyers have difficulty proving in court what they believe and know are fact. In the court of law, it is not what you tell the court you know and believe that will help you succeed, but what you can prove. What you know and believe but can't prove may not be considered by the court even when it is relevant to your case. Commonsense may not be relevant in legal issues.

We know how it goes when it comes to legal issues. Plaintiffs are to prove their case according to the rules of law and defendants are to defend themselves in a lawful manner. When it comes to legal issues, the stakes can be so high that no sides want to neither risk anything nor take any chances. When it comes to that, there may be the need of a lawyer's help. That is when the need of a lawyer comes into consideration. When you do not know how the court system works or the rules of law, it may not be a good idea to take the initiative of representing yourself in a civil or criminal case where the court procedures and process and the rules of law have to be followed properly. You may find yourself stuck and do not know precisely how to proceed and that is if you would know how to start in the first place. In some cases, judges and court personnel are not legally authorized to give legal advice to any party. A lawyer may be able to give you some legal advice in a specific legal matter, but may do little to help you fully and successfully represent yourself effectively in a case where the rules of law have to be properly followed if you were not trained to do so.

Lawyers try to defend cases at clients' own risk.

Even lawyers sometimes have trouble proving their case. They make claims based solely on speculation and lost cases. From today, before anybody else decides to represent himself in a court legal issue, he should know and understand that defendants and plaintiffs are to prove and defend their cases, make and defend claims according to the rules of law, and the court process and procedures are most likely to be followed properly.

Everyone tries to defend their case at their own risk. Lawyers try to defend cases at their clients' own risk. When it comes to criminal court, the system is so complicated and the criminal law and the court procedures and process have to be followed properly. In addition, the fact that it may involve jail or prison sentences is a good idea for anyone who is not properly trained as a lawyer to not try to represent themselves. Also consider the fact that even good lawyers with experience and who have been in practice for years sometimes lose criminal cases.

When being charged with a crime or when being treated as a suspect of a criminal act, one of the first things the accuser is thinking of is representation by a lawyer to defend them and protect their legal rights. In some cases, giving up of certain legal rights may lead to criminal charges. When it comes to criminal investigations and criminal charges, nobody wants to give up any legal rights that may lead to some consequences and, first of all, without talking to a lawyer. When investigators are interrogating a suspect about a crime and the suspect lies to them, the prosecutors may then try to prove their case to the jury at trial by trying to convince the jury that the defendant lied to them. Now the jury cannot believe or trust him and he should be held accountable at some point for the crime being accused of and be convicted when the lies of the defendants to the interrogators do not in fact prove or mean that he is the true offender of the crime. What the defendants tell interrogators may later be used against them during court procedures and at trial.

Defendants are most likely to deny charges against them, regardless of how guilty they truly are.

When someone is under criminal investigation and when being interrogated by investigators, he may be under a lot of pressure and is likely to say what he thinks may be able to save him from being charged including lies, even when he in fact knows that he is truly innocent and that he has nothing to hide. During the interrogation, he can be scared or precisely not remember things. Those signs may not always be signs of guilt. Also, the fact that the person knows that one of the reasons he is being interrogated as a suspect is because the investigators somehow believe that he may have something to do with the crime or know something about it. Sometimes, interrogators make the situation very difficult and confusing for the person they are interrogating with their flip-flop questions, regardless of how many explanations the suspect already gave them. Sometimes, they may keep on pushing to get the suspect to say what they want to hear from him to make their move against him, regardless of how irrelevant the suspect's answers might be. Sometimes, they base their questions to get precise answers in speculation and reference to what they want to hear and they will keep on asking and twist their questions until it comes to that. Therefore, when someone is faced with that kind of situation, they are more likely to seek a lawyer's help to help them fight the system and to help prove their innocence.

Keep in mind that some suspects or defendants, no matter how guilty they are of a crime, will try to do all they can to convince people that they are innocent. They act, speak, and behave as if they are truly innocent; they will not give up without a fight. They will do all they can to try to prove that the charges against them are false and they are most likely to hire a lawyer to try to prove the innocence of their guilt.

No matter how guilty a defendant might be of a crime, their lawyer is always going to try to prove the innocence of their guilt.

There is one thing lawyers have in common. When they have a consultation with a client, they are most likely to tell him that they can help him with his case, indirectly promising that they may be able to get the charges dropped or get the client acquitted just to be hired. That's before they even get to see the evidence and hear witness testimonies on the case. They make their assumption on hearing only one side of the story, the client's story.

In order to make the client comfortable and to win his confidence, they usually make a few phone calls in the presence of the client to the clerk of court to see what has been happening to the case, how far it has gotten, the next court date, and whatever else they deem appropriate. That is also to make the client believe that they will be very active on his case and that they will carry a fierce court battle if hired, even when that is not necessarily true. They are also most likely to cite some legal defense to the case according to the rules of law based on what the client told them. They do everything they can to gain the client's trust and confidence. Then they give him a price of how much it will cost for their representation. If agreed, then they have an agreement. It is then that problems start to happen between the lawyer and client.

Clients may want their lawyers to try their cases the clients' way, but their lawyers may refuse; they have to do it their way. Many clients do not understand that the criminal justice court system process and procedures do not go by what one wants to do or how they would like to defend their case, but what is allowed by law. The system's process and proceedings are very different from what one would like it to be. The system's process and procedures are to be followed properly by everyone, including lawyers. It is unfortunate that a client may want his lawyer to do or say something, show some evidence, present witnesses, or hear testimonies in a certain way, but because of the complexity of the criminal law, his lawyer cannot do it exactly as he wants it or as quickly as he would like.

Signs of suspect scariness at police interrogation does not necessarily mean guilt.

Through everything a lawyer has to do in a criminal case, including what his clients would like him to do, he has to do so according to the rules of law and follow court procedures properly. That sometimes restricts lawyers from personally doing what they or their clients would like them to do, which is not allowed by law.

A client can tell his lawyer he is innocent of a crime he is being accused of. He may know he is, his lawyer may believe he truly is, and he may convince the world that he really is, but when it comes to the court justice system, it is not something he just wants to say or wants his lawyer to prove however he deems necessary. It has to be done according to the rules of law and court process and procedures. If a client takes a case to a lawyer and would like the lawyer to prepare and present his defense the way the client wants, he is going to disagree a lot with his lawyer. They're going to have a lot of arguments and the client is going to have a lot of disappointment.

Sometimes, lawyers cannot get things done exactly the way their clients would like if it is not allowed by the rules of law. One of the best things a client can do is to tell his lawyer all he knows, gather all the evidence, alert him of all the witnesses, and make him aware of everything that is relevant to the case. The lawyer will make the determination of how to proceed properly. A client can communicate with his lawyer and ask him any questions he has. Clients should not be shy to ask their lawyers questions concerning their cases and all clients' questions are to be answered by their lawyers.

A defendant's way of seeing his case proceeding is not always what the law states.

It can be very frustrating for clients, so they ask their lawyers questions such as, "What is next?" "What do I expect from this point on?" "What will happen on the next court date?" "What will happen after my lawyer files papers or motions with the court?" "What will the chances of going to trial be?" "What should I expect when trial begins?"

A client must do all he can to not speak to anyone about his case without the presence or the consent of his lawyer. When it comes to questions concerning their cases, clients are going to have a lot of them. Because the system can be so confusing, most likely only lawyers, criminal justice system court personnel, and people who are relevantly trained understand it. Clients are going to have many questions about the ongoing process of their case, but also about how confusing the system is. A lawyer may have to explain everything to his client. I cannot tell you how many times I have heard clients asking their lawyers, "Why don't you do it this way instead?" And their lawyers responded, "Under what rules of law?"

Some clients blame their lawyers for losing their case because of their lawyer's refusal to present or defend their case the way *they* wanted. However, some of those clients fail to understand that sometimes their way of presenting and defending their case would not have been allowed, noticed, heard, or considered by the court because that would be contrary to what the rules of law say. I believe that if the defendant knows the court criminal justice system process and procedures and how to properly follow them, then he will not need a lawyer to represent him in the first place. Usually, a client's way of seeing things done by his lawyer in a criminal case is not always the lawful way of doing so.

Lawyers. You may dislike some of them, but when it comes to legal issues, they seem to come to our disposal and usually get our attention.

Lawyers are trained to do what they are doing. Sometimes they win and sometimes they lose cases and that is what most criminal cases that go to trial come to. Some lawyers may advise their clients to take or accept plea deals on criminal cases that their lawyers see has a small opportunity of winning. They will communicate with prosecutors on possible plea deals for their clients. Sometimes, defendants reject plea deals offered by the prosecutors on their criminal cases, but they must understand that while they may know that they are truly innocent of a criminal act they're being accused of, it is something that will need to be proven according to the rules of law.

A lawyer may believe that his client is innocent of a criminal act he is being accused of, but if there is no evidence strong enough to prove it, the lawyer then understands that there may not be a strong defense to that case. That may lead the lawyer to look for other ways to lessen the penalties for his client and that may direct the lawyer to look for a plea deal with the prosecution. The fact is that a criminal case with no strong defense can result in a conviction.

Prosecutors may sometimes do the same and offer a plea deal on a criminal case they see they do not have strong evidence against. The problem is, whether it is from the prosecutors or the defense, you cannot always speculate precisely on why they will want to offer or make a plea deal in every criminal case. Saying that the accused is innocent when he is not, the offender of the criminal acts being accused of may do too little to save a defendant from conviction if he cannot legally prove it. It can do little to help his lawyer prove his innocence and that's one of the reasons why defense lawyers make a determination for a plea deal on criminal cases against their clients.

In some cases and from a psychological point, being convicted of a crime may not necessarily mean nor prove that you committed it, but you were found guilty. When a lawyer communicates to his client about the possibility of cutting a plea deal with the prosecutors for the client's best interest in a criminal case, the client should ask his lawyer why and carefully consider all options. The client does not have to agree to take a plea deal on a criminal case against him; it is up to the client to make that determination. However, he must also consider the possibility of his lawyer not being able to fully or effectively prove his innocence at trial, which may result to some more serious consequences than taking a plea deal.

Defense lawyers usually have a better chance to work with the prosecutors to their clients' best interest if they agree to a plea deal, but that is less likely after conviction. No clients want to be convicted and face severe sentences in a criminal case where they have rejected their lawyers' request and advice for a plea deal. Some defendants may be less likely to agree to a plea deal in a criminal case against them when they know that they are innocent. A lawyer's request and advice of cutting a plea deal for a client's best interest sends a signal to the client that the lawyer may not be able to win at trial. However, that may not always be the case and this is why it is extremely important that a client must communicate with his lawyer. If a lawyer were not intending to cut a plea deal in a criminal case against his client, even if the prosecutors offered one, the lawyer must communicate to his client about the offer. If a plea deal is offered by the prosecutors, a lawyer, even if he is not suggesting his client take it, must make him aware of it and discuss all the options with him. A lawyer's advice to his client about cutting a plea deal with the prosecutors in a criminal case does not necessarily mean that the client has to do so.

Lawyers should make suggestions to benefit their clients. Lawyers make suggestions most likely to help their clients' cases whether some clients see it like that or not. We all have our differences and that also goes for clients and lawyers. However, some clients must do their best to understand that sometimes their lawyers' differences are in reflection of the rules of law.

We must continue to thank the law enforcement and the criminal justice system personnel for all their great effort and services. And also to continue to support and help them to always be successful on the difficult job they have to do day-by-day and with the prevention of criminal acts. They continue to put their lives on the line every day to protect ours. Let's give them credit for that and let them know that we appreciate them because they truly deserve it.

I myself personally thank them and congratulate them. Salute!

Chapter 5

Lawyers

Every criminal case somehow differs from each other in evidence, testimonies, witnesses, places, and time.

- Roldimy Montinar

As far as the court procedures and the rules of law are concerned, lawyers may continue to see things to be done differently from how some of their clients would like them to do so. Lawyers cannot try criminal cases however they want. They have court procedures to follow. The criminal court process and procedures and the criminal rules of law are to apply to criminal cases, tried by a lawyer or not. A client may see a criminal case to be defended differently than his lawyer's. However, if he was to represent himself, he may have had to follow the same procedure as his lawyer and do it his lawyer's way, which he had disagreed with in the first place.

It is not what you want to do but how you can do so lawfully. That is one of the reasons why some defendants, even when they know that they are innocent of a crime they are being charged with that they nor their lawyer cannot prove their innocence according to the rules of law. One of the problems lawyers have with their clients is the job being done and for how much. I cannot tell you how many times

I've heard people complaining about high legal costs and it seems like their lawyers are not really doing anything for what they're being paid.

Until their cases go to trial, most clients may see their lawyers filing papers with the court and the system moving slowly. In a court appearance, their lawyers only speak for a few minutes. Some clients sometimes argue that their lawyers are paid too much considering the amount of time they spend preparing their cases and the amount of time spent in court representing their clients in a criminal case. Sometimes, a lawyer in a criminal case may charge a client a flat fee rate to represent him based on prior experience with similar criminal cases.

Every single criminal case has its own circumstances.

Unfortunately, the flat fee may not cover everything and clients are most likely faced with additional fees as unexpected developments happen to their cases. A lawyer may not be able to tell his client how much time a criminal case will need until he talks with the prosecutors. It is then that they may have a better idea of what the evidence and who the witnesses are and how to prepare a successful defense for a client's case. Anything else that a lawyer may tell a client before that will more likely be speculation and assumption based on what the client told him and evidence he presents him with at the time of the consultation.

A criminal case that a lawyer believes might last six months may end up lasting more than that and that can result in additional fees. When a lawyer charges a client a flat fee to defend him, the lawyer is more likely to take short cuts and insist on having the case finished sooner than later. Lawyers give services to what their clients pay for, which means that another client who has the same kind of case as you may end up getting better services and defense from your lawyer than you do if he pays more than you do.

When a lawyer charges a flat fee to represent a client in a criminal case, he is more likely to rush the process and the client may not get the best possible defense or services he should have. Some lawyers give fair or good services and defense if the clients pay them less or more. When they charge a flat fee, they are more likely not to spend a lot of time on a case preparing it. They will defend their clients, but the services they give a client may be poor considering if the client would have paid more money for the same service.

Best service and defense from a lawyer does not always guarantee "acquittance" in a criminal case.

A lawyer may rush a client's case and avoid spending overtime on it if he will not be paid for the extra time. The client may not get the benefit of the best defense he should have received. There have been cases where a lawyer had not spent enough time on a client's case preparing it for a court date and will try to do so hours before a court appearance. There have been cases where a lawyer went to court, but forgot important paperwork about a client's case. There also have been cases where a lawyer forgets to file important paperwork with the court about a client's case. There had been a case where a lawyer went to court to defend a client's case, but was unprepared to do so. He put the court on hold looking for his papers, asking for unnecessary continuance, and getting everybody aggravated. Keep in mind that some lawyers when they charge a client a flat fee to represent him in a criminal case, will give the client services and defense fair to what he pays for. The better defense a client needs, the more money he may have to pay his lawyer. Keep in mind that that may not always be the case. When a client pays a lawyer to defend him, it does not mean that the client will receive the best services and defense possible for his money from that lawyer. The better services and defense a client may need, the more willful he may want to be about going beyond the flat fee charges, which could mean additional fees. However, at the same time, a client in a criminal case may pay a simple flat fee charge and get better services and defense than another client who paid the big bucks for the same services and defense and by the same lawyer.

Some clients get charged constantly by their lawyers in a criminal case. They may pay a retainer fee and every single time their lawyers have to do something, they get charged for it. Usually, those clients end up paying more than some of those who just pay the flat fee rate. They most likely end up getting better services and defense and their lawyers may decide to proceed slowly with their cases. The more time a client's case takes, the more time their lawyers spend on their cases, the more services are given, the more paperwork, the more court appearances, and then the more money it will cost the client.

A client's ability to pay a lawyer more than others in a criminal case may result in him getting better services and defense than the others do.

They may in fact get the best services and defense from their lawyers because they pay more for them. It may happen that a client who pays big bucks for a criminal case gets the same service as another client who just pays a flat fee charge for the same kind of case and with the same lawyer.

There have been cases where some of those who pay the big bucks to their lawyers for representation end up cutting a plea deal with the prosecutors. Paying big bucks to a lawyer may not save a client from conviction. Paying big bucks to a lawyer may somehow guarantee the best services and the best possible defense from that lawyer, but it does not guarantee acquittance in a criminal case. Sometimes, the outcome of a criminal case may not depend on how much more or less a client pays his lawyer for his services or how weak or strong his defense was presented by his lawyer. Even the best services and defense from a lawyer does not always guarantee acquittance in a criminal case.

A client's ability and capability to pay a lawyer more than others does not always mean he will receive better services or defense than the others in a criminal case. When a client pays a lawyer for his services and to defend him, he can only assume that he will receive the best services and defense from that lawyer. However, the client does not know for sure nor does he have any guarantee if that will be the case.

There is one thing lawyers have in common. When somebody takes a criminal case to them, they sometimes try to put other lawyers down and want to make that person believe and try to prove that they can do better. They will try to convince that person that they are the best in town and the best for his case. They will try to do everything within their power to win that person's trust and to make him believe in them. They will tell that person that they have represented other clients on similar cases and their cases were dropped, dismissed, or they were acquitted.

A client must earn a lawyer's trust.

Some people take those comments directly and think if they hire that lawyer, their cases will be dismissed or they will be acquitted. Some lawyers will most likely tell you how many similar cases like yours they have won, but they will barely tell you how many they have lost if asked. Some lawyers will tell their clients that they can help them, but some clients consider that as seeing the criminal cases against them being dismissed or acquitted. Some lawyers in their advertisements say how many years of experience they have. Some people consider a lawyer's years of experience as seeing their criminal case dismissed or acquitted if they hire that lawyer. Unfortunately, a lawyer's years of experience does not always guarantee that.

When a person presents a lawyer with a criminal case and the lawyer says that he can help, that does not mean that he will be able to successfully get that person acquitted or get the charges against him dropped. That is how some of them want to make it sound and some people believe them. Upon consultation, some lawyers are most likely to say all kinds of things to a person to win that person's trust and get him to retain them. A client must earn a lawyer's trust. To a client, the best defense by his lawyer must not be assumed, but be proven.

To a client, the best defense by his lawyer must not be assumed, but be proven.

Even those who are considered the best lawyers cannot always guarantee case dismissal of acquittance to everyone who walks into their office with a criminal case. However, they can provide the best defense possible that can result to that. Chances are, when a person takes a criminal case to a lawyer, upon consultation, that person will get to hear only the good things about that lawyer even if there isn't any. It is a game some lawyers play to get cases and to win a client's confidence. Sometimes, that can lead to trouble between some lawyers and clients. Some clients further down the road find out that all the good things they heard about their lawyers by their lawyers and all their promises given did not guarantee dismissal of their cases. That can cause arguments between some clients and their lawyers.

Some lawyers are cautious about directly saying to anyone who brings a criminal case to their office, upon consultation, that they will get the criminal case against him dismissed or get him acquitted. Upon consultation, some lawyers do not always like to tell a person the whole truth about the possibility of the outcome of their cases. The whole truth is upon consultation; it is just too early for any lawyer to know if he will be able to do just that. While a lawyer might give a criminal case against his client the best possible defense and do his best, the charges being dropped depends on the prosecutor, the dismissal of a criminal case depends on the court criminal justice system personnel, and an acquittance is in the hands of the jury. Some lawyers will tell their clients that after they get their money.

Some lawyers usually do not tell their clients the whole truth about the possibility of the outcome of the criminal cases against them until after they are paid.

A lawyer who makes a client so confident that he will be able to do this and that in a criminal case may later, after he gets the client's money, change his story and tell his client that he really does not have the authority to get his case dropped or get him acquitted (as he thought), but it is up to the court, the prosecutors, and the jury. Even when a lawyer sees there is no good defense for a criminal case against his client, he may wait until he is paid to make his client aware of that. It does not matter how much some may hate some lawyers, but when it comes to legal issues, they seem to come to our consideration and usually get our attention.

Lawyers use certain means to win a client's confidence to retain them. Some lawyers get a client's money first before they tell him that they will give him the best services and provide him with the best possible defense, but they cannot guarantee that will automatically get the criminal case against him dismissed or get him acquitted. In some cases, lawyers do not have the authority to drop charges against their clients, but they can do their best to get it accomplished. It is up to the court, the prosecutors, and the jury to decide a defendant's acquittance or the dismissal of his case; some defense lawyers can play a role in that also, but they may not have the authority to do so. If they did, then every single criminal case against their clients would have been dismissed automatically. Some have said that some lawyers are not honest. Others have said they do not trust some lawyers. I believe they have their own reasons for saying so. You may not want, as a client, to argue representation fee with your lawyer considering the fact that you may receive services only fair to what you agree to pay. Also, paying a lawyer big bucks does not always guarantee the best services. However, a client may not want to neglect the best defense to a criminal case against him for trying to pay his lawyer less than his recommended fees.

It is one thing lawyers have in common to disagree with their opponent's claims.

If a lawyer tells a client he will charge him X amount of dollars to represent him in a criminal case, the client might be better off finding another lawyer who will give him the same kind of service and defense or better for less money than trying to tell his lawyer his fees are too high.

A lawyer who charges his client for the best service may then give his client fair service if the lawyer has to lower his fees. A lowering in price and fees may also lower the quality of the services given. It may not always be a good idea for a client to argue with his lawyer about the lawyer's recommended fees to represent the client in a criminal case considering the fact that the client may only get services valued to what he pays for them.

Some lawyers do not tell their clients what kind of service they will give their clients for what they charge them or for what their clients agree to pay, but the clients can only assume that the services will be the best; however, that may not always be the case. Paying big bucks for legal representation on criminal cases may not always get a client the best defense possible from his lawyer. A lawyer may charge a client just a little bit of money to represent him in a criminal case and give him the best possible defense that would have cost the client some big bucks.

Lawyers are sensible about being paid when due by their clients.

Some lawyers may give you the same quality of service, regardless of how much less or more you pay them. Some others may give their clients services to what their money is worth. They will give better services if their clients pay more and provide average service if their clients pay them less. A client may never want to come in conflict with his lawyer for not being able or not be willing to pay his lawyer for his representation and services in a criminal case. Before the client knows it, he may see a motion from his lawyer to withdraw from his case. No matter how good a lawyer is, regardless of how fair or unfair he might be with the kind of services given, a client may never want to be dishonest with his lawyer when it comes to paying him and on time for his continuous representation if the client would like to receive the best possible defense from his lawyer.

Lawyers are very sensible about being paid when due by their clients. Before hiring a lawyer in a criminal case, a client must know what kind of services and the quality of defense he will receive for what he is paying. A client is to make that determination before he hires any lawyer. A client may not want the quality and the kind of services he will get from a lawyer to be measured in differences of how much more the client pays, but to always receive the best possible services from that lawyer, regardless of how much less the client pays in differences.

The quality of services and the kind of defense a lawyer gives his clients should not be measured by how much more or less the clients pay for them.

One may argue that good lawyers provide good services to their clients. Where there is some truth to that, it may not always be the case. A good lawyer may charge a client for the best possible services he can provide upon consultation, but if the client wants to work with the kind of services he wants, he may be able to do so and make his own offer to the lawyer. In this case, the lawyer may accept the lower offer than his suggested fees. Keep in mind though that that may also lower the quality of services the client may receive. A client may go from getting the best possible defense to just average considering what he agrees to pay his lawyer. A lawyer may be able to provide a client with the best possible services available. However, it is not a given that a good lawyer will always provide the best services to his clients.

A good lawyer can decide when to give a client his best services or not. Moreover, that can be measured by how much more or less the clients agree to pay. Good lawyers may not always give the best services possible to all their clients or to everyone who walks into their offices with a case. The kind of services a client receives from his lawyer can be measured by how much they pay for them. It is as if the lawyer put a price to the quality of services he provides and a client can choose what kind of services he wants by giving a reasonable offer.

Almost everything a lawyer does to a client's criminal case during court proceedings may become relevant to the outcome of the case.

For example. Best service = $5.00; Better service = $4.00; Good service = $3.00; Average service = $2.00. The dollar amount is just a figure for example only. When a client walks into a lawyer's office with a case, the lawyer is most likely to charge him for the best service, but the client can reject that and make his own reasonable offer that may lower the quality of service all the way down to just average. When it is time to hire a lawyer, a client should think wisely about those possibilities. The fact that when lawyers charge their clients for their services, they may never tell the clients if they may lower the quality of services if the clients choose to pay less than what the lawyers suggested. While a client may never know in advance of what kind of services he will get from his lawyer, the client always wants to make sure that his lawyer understands that the client only wants to work with a lawyer who will provide him with the best possible services for what he agrees to pay. He simply does not just want to trust his lawyer; he must earn the lawyer's trust and confidence. He must prove to the client that the choice he made by hiring him was not a mistake and to give the client reason to always be his first consideration for future cases. The lawyer's honesty should not be proven by words, but by action.

If a client does not trust a lawyer, the client thinks the lawyer is dishonest. The best thing to do is for the client not to hire that lawyer no matter how good the client might think he is. For the simple fact that the client may always have some doubt in that lawyer and questioning his services even when the lawyer is providing the client with the best possible services available. And that may lead to some conflict between them on how differently each one of them sees the case to proceed.

Lawyers try criminal cases at their clients' own risk.

One other factor to consider is that lawyers try criminal cases at their clients' own risk. Almost everything a lawyer does to a client's criminal case during court proceedings may become relevant to the outcome of the case.

When a client presents a criminal case to a lawyer, upon consultation, the lawyer can tell the client whatever he wants or make any kind of promises he would like, but he certainly cannot promise or proclaim the acquittance of the client at that early time. That is to be decided as the case proceeds.

When a client hires a lawyer to represent him in a criminal case, he does not do so with the only option that he will be acquitted, but he is hopeful that the lawyer will provide him with necessary defense that leads to there. If a client is to take a criminal case to any lawyer with the only option that they promise the client's acquittance, upon consultation, for the client to retain any of them, chances are that client may not find even one lawyer who will take his case. Some of them may, but lawyers do not usually make those kinds of promises at consultation time. If a lawyer should make such a promise to a client upon consultation, then the client must ask that lawyer that he do so in writing and sign it. At consultation, it can be too early for a lawyer to say precisely what will happen to a criminal case.

Lawyers. It is their profession that makes them act like enemies, but they are truly professional friends.

At consultation, a lawyer usually gets to hear only one side of the story in a criminal case. The defendant's side has no idea yet of what kind of evidence the prosecutors may have, their witnesses, or their side of the story. A lawyer must file papers with the court to get that info and that can sometimes take a little time to receive them. Until that time, any word from a lawyer about the outcome of a client's case can be just assumption.

One of a client's best chances can be when his lawyer knows the prosecution team very well and can successfully work with them. However, prosecutors are not always to drop charges against a defendant simply because the defendant's lawyer asks them to do so in a friendly or a professional way. That may sometimes be the case but not always. Some clients see problems with their lawyers being friendly with the prosecution's team. It may only be when they face each other in court that they act like enemies, but beyond that, they act like professionals and in a friendly manner. They have to work through their differences, the prosecutors to prove the defendant's guilt and defense criminal lawyers to prove their client's innocence. The criminal justice system usually allows them to do that in a professional way. Being realistic, criminal defense lawyers and prosecutors being very friendly with each other can bring some good or bad news to some criminal cases. Today, prosecutors have a defense lawyer do a favor on a particular criminal case and tomorrow, the defense lawyer will return the favor to the prosecutors on that criminal case. Sometimes, that can bring unfortunate consequences to a criminal case. The result of those fortunate or unfortunate consequences by a client lawyer's behavior will be at the client's own risk. There have been cases where some lawyers lose their client's case because they did not provide enough effort of the defense required from their part. There have been cases where some lawyers' own mistakes led to some unfortunate consequence or outcome.

I believe that there are some courageous and trusted lawyers with integrity and honesty out there, but some clients hope all would be like that.

When a client hires a lawyer in a criminal case, it means the client trusts that lawyer with his case; the client gives him the power to act on his behalf in the case and to defend the client. Before a client retains a lawyer in a criminal case, he should first question the lawyer's ability and capability of bringing the outcome of the case the client wants. The decision to hire a lawyer should not solely be based on unsure promises and assumption. A lawyer should be hired with careful consideration, qualification, and experience, even when that does not always guarantee good news to every criminal case.

In a criminal case, a client can have so much at stake: his life and his freedom. The outcome can include jail or prison sentences. One of the things clients do when they hire a lawyer to represent them in a criminal case is that they give their lawyers the power to defend them at their own risk and at the fortunate or unfortunate outcome of their cases. On the other hand, lawyers should understand that when their clients give them all that to defend, it should not be taken lightly and to provide their clients with the best defense and services possible. I believe that there are some courageous and trusted lawyers with integrity and honesty out there, but some clients hope that all would be like that. That is the kind of lawyers a client would always like to work with.

The fact is that when some people talk about a particular group of lawyers, they usually refer to all of them. It is possible that those honest lawyers will continue to be hurt when it comes to criticism.

I have heard some people criticizing lawyers and others say they hate them even when they have to work with them. Even though some people make bad comments about a lawyer, they may have their reasons to do so, but I will pray for every lawyer out there to always do the best they can to earn their client's trust, to prove to their clients their honesty, to always give them the best possible defense and services, to always treat all of them fairly, to always give them the best representation, to always meet and exceed their expectations, to work their cases toward successful desired outcomes, to always give them the best quality of services, to always be honest with them, to be courageous with their cases, to always use tremendous effort to satisfy them, to always bring satisfaction to their cases, and to always make the outcome of their cases a complete success.

Some clients may then have a better experience with their lawyers and that may help some lawyers to clean up their acts. When some people talk about a particular group of lawyers, they usually refer to all of them. Therefore, it is possible that some honest lawyers will continue to be hurt by what some dishonest lawyers do when it comes to criticism. Keep in mind that I am not personally accusing any lawyer of being dishonest.

Before hiring a criminal lawyer to represent you in a criminal case, you should first think about the kind of responsibility you are putting into the hands of that lawyer. Think of the possible consequences that can result in some weak defense and services from him. Think about the risk involved having a lawyer acting on your behalf. Think of the fact that no matter how innocent you know you are, it is somehow the responsibility of that lawyer to prove it. Think of the fact that a lawyer's own mistakes can result in your conviction. Consider those facts and factors carefully, and then decide who you really want to hire as your lawyer and give all those responsibilities to. Keep in mind that lawyers are to defend you in a criminal case and collect money for their services. They will defend you at your own risk and whatever the outcome of your case, they may not have anything to lose.

Clients can only hope that will be the case. As I see it, clients only pay their defense criminal lawyers to defend them on criminal charges against them, but not to automatically get them acquitted of them.

A lawyer who recklessly loses a client's criminal case may feel sorry to see that client being sentenced to jail for his own error, but he will not help share the burden he costs that client for his mistake.

There have been cases where some lawyers feel sorry to see their clients convicted for a crime the lawyers personally believe their clients are innocent of. However, they just could not prove it or they could not convince the jury. Still, they just feel sorry for those clients, but they will not refund their money nor help them share their sentences.

I have heard some people suggesting that when a lawyer loses a client's criminal case, he should refund some of the money he charged the client to represent him. I believe that when a client went to a lawyer's office with a criminal case, if hired, he retained that lawyer to represent him and defend him, but not to directly and automatically get him acquitted. He pays the lawyer for his services and to defend him, but the services of the lawyer and the defense he provides does not mean and does not guarantee the client's acquittal of any charges against him.

If a client hires a lawyer to represent him in a criminal case with the condition to successfully get the client's case dismissed or gets him acquitted of any charges against him, and that lawyer positively agrees to that with no exception at all, but he fails to do so, then that is a different story. The fact is when a client hires a lawyer to represent him in a criminal case, that client does so and pays the lawyer for his services and to defend him. Hopefully, the lawyer's services will lead to case dismissal or acquittance.

One who dares to say he never violated the criminal law once during his lifetime dares to say he never sins.

In some cases, some of those who are charged with a crime and cannot financially afford to hire a lawyer of their choice to represent them may have the possibility of having the criminal court judicial system appoint a lawyer to them. In some cases, a defendant must apply to receive that service and must be qualified for it. Many defendants who get court appointed lawyers to represent them in criminal cases do not trust them at all considering the fact that they are working for the same system that is trying to convict them. If a defendant in a criminal case is to hire a lawyer of their choice, they are more likely to retain one they believe will give them the best possible service and defense available. One can argue that, if a court is to appoint a lawyer to a defendant's case, that court should make sure that that defendant receives the best possible services and defense available.

Every defendant is entitled to receive the best defense and services from his lawyer. Many defendants feel like court appointed lawyers are sometimes unable to do that considering the load of cases they may have at once and the limited resources provided to them. It sometimes makes it very difficult for them to spend the amount of time required on each of their clients' case to provide them with the best possible services and defense. Court appointed lawyers might have so many cases at once that they may have a hard time keeping track of them. How can a lawyer provide the best services and provide the best possible defense to his clients if he is having a hard time keeping track of all his cases? Not everyone who is charged with a crime will be able to hire his own lawyer to defend them, so they will have to rely on court appointed lawyers. The fact that a court appointed lawyer is working for the same system that is trying to get the defendant convicted, many clients think if they say something to their court appointed lawyers, it is like telling it to the prosecution's team.

The criminal law is not to be used nor applied in two contrary and conflicted ways, but only one and that is for what it states.

Can you imagine working with a lawyer in a criminal case against you who you do not trust at all? One can argue that if a court is to provide the service of a lawyer to anyone who cannot afford to hire one of their own, that court should and must make sure that that person is to be beneficial of the best services and defense possible a lawyer could have provided him with. A client who is represented by a court appointed lawyer might tell his appointed lawyer of some evidence that may be helpful in their case, but lacks the resources and money to do so.

There are certain procedures that a court appointed lawyer might not be able to go beyond. Court appointed lawyers should receive all the resources and money necessary to pursue and prove their client's innocence. Some prosecution's team may oppose because they most likely do not want some defendants to be provided with the best possible defense, so they can be convicted. Therefore, some prosecutors may oppose the approval of necessary money and resources to a public defender vital for him to prove his client's innocence in a criminal case against him.

What some prosecutors are looking for is for some defendants not to get the best defense possible, but to be convicted. They will most likely do what they can to oppose all that and that is contrary to what they are pushing for. Some defendants do not trust court appointed lawyers. They would rather risk their cases and refuse the services of any court appointed lawyer to their case, and try to represent themselves. They will not talk to them, as they should have done because they believe it is a waste of time.

It is wrong for a lawyer to provide his client with limited defense in a criminal case.

There is a lot court appointed lawyers have to do to successfully defend their clients, but unfortunately, sometimes what they are allowed to do is limited. No clients and defendants should be given just limited defense from any lawyer. It is wrong for a lawyer to provide his clients with limited defense in a criminal case. Sometimes, a lawyer will really need to go beyond that limited defense to successfully prove a client's innocence in a criminal case against him. Sometimes, limited defense can be like no defense at all. Some defense is not always the best defense possible.

When a court appointed lawyer represents a defendant in a criminal case, his services and quality of defense provided can have a lot to do with the outcome of the case. Considering that and the possibility of jail or prison sentences if convicted, why should any defendant receive just limited defense from his lawyer?

Some criminal defense lawyers are happy with the fact that some defendants do not trust court appointed lawyers and may not want to work with them. Their services and defense provided can be limited, considering the fact that some of those defendants may end up hiring a lawyer of their choice in hopes to receive the best possible defense. If court appointed lawyers were always to give the best possible services to their clients and provide them with the best available defense, then some criminal defense lawyers would have been left fishing for clients. Some criminal defense lawyers know that and that is one of the reasons some of them may continue to support the limited services and defense to some defendants from some court appointed lawyers. It is not that they do not know that it is wrong, but they will not criticize it considering the fact that it may cost them clients if court appointed lawyers were to always provide to their clients the same or better services than those lawyers.

Loyal lawyers know that their clients must earn their trust. Their honesty and integrity must be an example and that their clients' confidence in them must never be allowed to be questioned.

Keep in mind that I am not at all saying that it is always the case that defendants in criminal cases receive limited services and defense from their court appointed lawyers. The court and the criminal judicial system should always make sure that all defendants receive the best services and defense from their court appointed lawyers. Moreover, if they are to appoint a court appointed lawyer to a defendant's criminal case, they are to make sure of that. It would be wrong for a court to appoint a lawyer to a defendant's case with the intention for that defendant to receive limited services and defense from that lawyer. If that should ever be the case, then one can argue that the court intentionally sought the conviction of that defendant if convicted. If a court should intentionally allow his court appointed lawyers to provide limited services and defense to their clients, but not what is vital, necessary, and required by law to prove their innocence if they are, then one can argue that the court somehow pursued and sought the conviction of those clients if convicted and may also have abused their rights under the law.

One can argue that when defendants are charged with a crime and do not have money to hire their own personal lawyers to defend them and when conviction can result to life in prison or the death penalty sentence, then instead of court appointed lawyers, courts should appoint to those defendants any affordable lawyers out there of their choice at the court's expense that they feel comfortable working with. They need to trust them and believe they will give them the best services and provide them with the best possible defense. One may argue that that would be a waste of taxpayers' money. Others may argue that considering the fact that every defendant in a criminal case should be given the best possible services and be provided with the best possible defense, it would be a fair action and that the criminal court judicial system personnel should take it under consideration. Others may argue that such action would be unfair if it should only be applied to those who were faced with the ultimate sentence if convicted. If it is applied to one criminal case, then it should be applied to all criminal cases. One may argue that such action may encourage some to commit crime knowing that they will be given the option of hiring any affordable lawyers of their choice even if they cannot afford it and that might give a boost to crime rates. One may argue that if that ever happens to be the case, those defendants should be held responsible to pay back that money, regardless of the outcome of their cases. Those fees can add up to so much that it may take some defendants' years to pay them off.

One may argue that a defendant who gets the ultimate sentence may be careless about paying any legal fees back. One may also argue that when a defendant is acquitted of a criminal charge against him or a criminal case against him is dismissed, he should be entitled to be reimbursed for all his expenses occurring during his case. One can also argue that the law should provide thorough penalties to any prosecutor who unlawfully prosecutes any criminal case. One can argue that there should be laws to prosecute and punish criminal prosecution personnel for every time they willfully and unlawfully prosecute anybody for a crime he did not commit when they in fact know that they had the wrong person and had evidence to prove it. One can argue that doing so may help with some criminal prosecution personnel to stop making people victims of their injustice and the act of unlawful prosecution and wrongful conviction.

Justice for victim of injustice.

One can argue that if some criminal prosecution personnel know that there will be some serious consequences for unlawful acts and behavior, they will most likely stop abusing what the law says and stop using it for their own interest.

I believe that everyone should receive the best services and be provided with the best possible defense by their lawyer or by their court appointed lawyer. People should only be charged and prosecuted for crimes they have committed and should only be convicted of crimes they are truly guilty of. The criminal law should always and only be used for what it states and the criminal law should always be applied for what it says, *Justice for all,* and that is with no exception. The law should always be used in a fair way and lawful to all of us.

A Letter from the Author

Expert criminal studies are lacking precise location, time, and evidence to always be able to tell accurately when and how someone will break the criminal law. There are so many experts out there studying crime, why they happen, and how to help prevent them prematurely. While they have had some success, it is not always a total complete success on all crimes. No matter where you live in the world, crime continues to lighten itself every day.

I have read reports of certain regions of the world where they had either a low or a lower crime rate. However, lower crime rates tell you that crime does happen in those regions and they are not crime free. No matter how much explanation we have been given about crime, what best to do to prevent it, regardless of the great effort of the law enforcement personnel, the toughness of the criminal justice system on those who commit unlawful acts, and despite the ongoing crime experts' studies and findings, people continue to violate the criminal law. One of the reasons is because we all have the ability and the capability to violate the criminal law and sometimes nobody else can control our ability or capability to do so but ourselves. We all have the ability and the capability to do so, regardless of what the criminal law says, stands for, and is against because some people do commit criminal acts anyway even when they know their acts will break the criminal law in the first place.

The criminal law itself, despite what it states, cannot stop people from violating it. We all have a great job to do when it comes to helping with the prevention of crime. We all need to have respect for the criminal law and to not violate it. We all need to act responsibly and think about what we want to do before we do it. We need to avoid doing what can lead to the violation of the criminal law and think about the consequences of committing criminal acts. We should always act with justice.

We all need not to behave criminally, have respect for the criminal law, and act accordingly, and that can help with the prevention of crime. If nobody commits criminal acts, then the criminal law will not be violated.

Every time somebody becomes a victim of a crime, it means that someone had violated the criminal law. We all need to act responsibly so that no one becomes a victim of another's crime and to do the best we can to make the world a crime free place. Together we can do it. I believe that if we are all committed to it, we can make it happen.

We can make sure that no criminal law is broken again and we can help do that by not, first of all, violating it ourselves. The ability, the capability, and motives to break the criminal law are within our control and ourselves. We do not automatically break the criminal law, but we usually choose to do so. By doing so, some cause others to become victims of their criminal acts. No one should do that to others because I believe that none of us would like to become victims of others' criminal and irresponsible acts. Unless we are determined not to break the criminal law, there is little the law enforcement or the criminal justice system personnel can do to help prevent every single crime because they do not have total control over every single person's ability and capability to break the criminal law and motives that can lead to do so.

Despite their great job and effort, I believe that they cannot fight the battle against crime by themselves and they need every single person's help and cooperation in their fight against crime and to prevent it.

When we help the law enforcement and the criminal justice system personnel in their battle against crime, we also help others and ourselves from becoming victims of criminal acts. And for that, we will be very grateful whether or not single thanks were said to us for our great effort. We all have a job to do, and let's always act lawfully and responsibly to others.

We must continue to thank the law enforcement and the criminal justice system personnel for all their great effort and services. And also to continue to support and help them to always be successful on the difficult job they have to do day-by-day and with the prevention of criminal acts. They continue to put their lives on the line every day to protect ours. Let's give them credit for that and let them know that we appreciate them because they truly deserve it.

I myself personally thank them and congratulate them. Salute!

Roldimy Montinar

About the Author

Roldimy Montinar was born in St. Marc, Haiti. He attended Ecole Frere Herve (elementary and middle school) and Lycee Stenio Vincent (high school) both in St. Marc, Haiti, and Naples High School (high school) in Florida, USA. He then went on to attend The University of Phoenix, Edison State College, and Ashford University.

In 2004, he published his first book entitled *Succeed Financially and be Debt Free.*

Special Thanks:

Many continuous special thanks to everyone especially you, to my strong, lovely mother, to my brothers and sisters, to all my family, to all my friends, to all my advisors, to all my teachers, to my loving son: Alexander, to the editor, to my loving wife: Shenique and family, to Jurolien Jean Paul and family. There are too many to list. I thank GOD especially because without Him, this book would have never become a reality and a success.

Thank you so much.

Roldimy Montinar.

Made in the USA
Monee, IL
08 November 2026

67378679R00052